Elements of Lite...

Holt Adapted Reader

Answer Key

HOLT, RINEHART AND WINSTON

A Harcourt Education Company

Orlando • **Austin** • New York • San Diego • Toronto • London

CREDITS

Executive Editors: Juliana Koenig, Katie Vignery

Senior Editors: Susan Kent Cakars, Leslie Griffin, Marcia L. Kelley

Copyediting: Michael Neibergall, *Copyediting Manager;* Kristen Azzara, Mary Malone, *Copyediting Supervisors;* Christine Altgelt, Elizabeth Dickson, Leora Harris, Anne Heausler, Kathleen Scheiner, *Senior Copyeditors;* Emily Force, Julia Thomas Hu, Nancy Shore, *Copyeditors*

Project Administration: Marie Price, *Managing Editor;* Elizabeth LaManna, *Associate Managing Editor;* Janet Jenkins, Erik Netcher, *Senior Editorial Coordinators;* Christine Degollado, Betty Gabriel, Mark Koenig, *Editorial Coordinators*

Permissions: Ann Farrar, *Senior Permissions Editor;* Sally Garland, Susan Lowrance, *Permissions Editors*

Design: Betty Mintz, Richard Metzger, *Design Directors;* Chris Smith, *Senior Designer;* Peter Sawchuk, *Designer*

Production: Beth Prevelige, *Senior Production Manager;* Carol Trammel, *Production Manager;* Dolores Keller, Belinda Barbosa Lopez, Carol Marunas, Michael Roche, *Senior Production Coordinators;* Myles Gorospe, *Production Assistant*

Manufacturing: Shirley Cantrell, *Manufacturing Supervisor;* Mark McDonald, *Inventory Analyst;* Amy Borseth, *Manufacturing Coordinator*

0-03-035911-2

8 9 10 11 018 10 09 08

CONTENTS

A Guide to Using *Holt Adapted Reader*

Answer Key to the Student Editions

Welcome to the Program

Holt Adapted Reader is a consumable paperback book designed to accompany *Elements of Literature*. In addition to original selections, this text includes numerous selections whose vocabulary and sentence structure have been adapted to make stories and articles more accessible to struggling readers. *Holt Adapted Reader* offers scaffolded instruction in the reading process and encourages students to become active readers by circling, underlining, questioning, and jotting down responses as they read.

Students who need extra support while working in the main anthology will find that using *Holt Adapted Reader* helps them move with the rest of the class in discussions, writing assignments, and projects. One type of extra support is the simplified phonetic pronunciations of difficult words. To make these pronunciations even more accessible to students, you may wish to hand out photocopies of the Pronunciation Guide on page *xiv*.

Holt Adapted Reader can be used for independent practice. Clear directions, uncomplicated format, and consistent instruction make this book an ideal tool for effective homework or for students who need additional help.

This Program Includes

- *Holt Adapted Reader*, Student Edition
- *Holt Adapted Reader*, Answer Key

A Walk Through *Holt Adapted Reader*

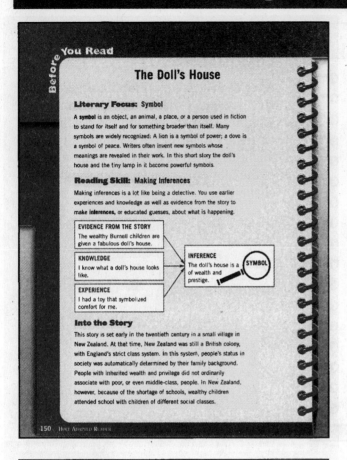

Prereading

The **Before You Read** page previews the skills students will practice as they read the selection.

- In the **Literary Focus,** students will learn about a literary element—such as character or rhyme—that they will see in the selection.
- The **Reading Skill** presents a key skill students will need to read the selection.

The **Before You Read** page also introduces students to the reading selection.

- **Into the Story** gives them background information on the selection, its author, or the time period in which the story, play, essay, poem, or article was written.

During Reading

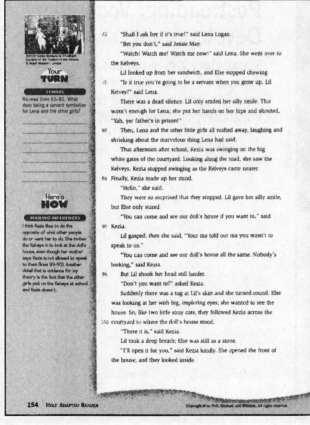

The **Here's HOW** feature shows students how to apply a particular skill to what they are reading. This feature models how another person might think about the text. Each Here's HOW focuses on a reading skill, a literary skill, or a vocabulary skill.

The **Your TURN** feature gives students a chance to practice a reading, literary, or vocabulary skill on their own. Students might be asked to underline or circle words in the text or to write their responses in the side margin.

A Walk Through *Holt Adapted Reader*

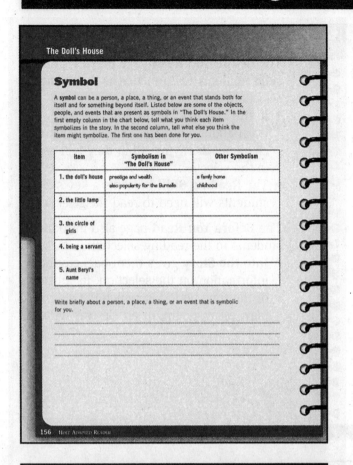

Postreading: Graphic Organizers

After each selection, **graphic organizers** give students a visual way to organize, interpret, and understand the reading skill or literary focus of the selection. Students might be asked to chart the main events of the plot or complete a cause-and-effect chain.

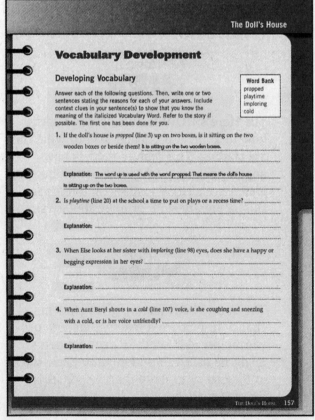

Postreading: Vocabulary Development

Vocabulary Development worksheets at the end of some selections reinforce selection vocabulary and teach new vocabulary acquisition skills.

Guiding Principles

Holt Adapted Reader

1. The differentiated instruction in *Holt Adapted Reader* assists struggling readers in comprehending grade-level instruction. Using adaptations of selections found in *Elements of Literature*, these students will be able to participate more fully in class discussion and activities with their peers.

2. Struggling readers need explicit and systematic reading instruction. *Holt Adapted Reader* provides scaffolded instruction, including modeling, to guide students through the reading process. This text focuses on reading strategies that effective readers use: identify, retell, infer, predict, interpret, evaluate, visualize, compare and contrast, connect, and acquire new vocabulary. Repetition of these strategies with a variety of text structures helps students develop effective reading habits and gain confidence with texts that are accessible.

3. Struggling readers need a wide range of texts to become comfortable reading both in and out of school. Students read a variety of literature in the context of historical and social development.

4. Direct interaction with text helps struggling readers make a more personal connection to the text. Students underline, circle, comment, and respond at the point they encounter text.

5. *Holt Adapted Reader* is designed to be used in a variety of instructional situations—with individuals, small groups, or the whole class—to provide teachers with the flexibility needed to use the program with all students.

On the following pages is a discussion of the core instructional strategies in *Holt Adapted Reader* and some ideas for extending these strategies into your classroom.

Even if you are not a trained reading teacher, there are numerous excellent reading strategies you can use to help struggling readers in your classroom. The instruction in the *Holt Adapted Reader* program is based on two of the best ways to improve students' reading comprehension—modeling thinking aloud and building student fluency.

Think-Alouds

In a Think-Aloud, students pause in their reading from time to time to think aloud about what connections they are making to the text, what images they see, what questions they have, and how they might answer them. This strategy allows you to understand where a student is having difficulty, and it helps the student analyze his or her own reading process. **Here's HOW** features in *Holt Adapted Reader* model thinking aloud for students. These features, written from a student's perspective, show how a good reader might apply a particular reading, literary, or vocabulary skill to the text. **Your TURN** features then invite students to practice these skills on their own.

You can build on the instruction in *Holt Adapted Reader* by practicing Think-Alouds in the classroom. To model a Think-Aloud, tell students that you will be reading aloud and stopping from time to time to think about what you have just read. As you read to the class, stop often to talk about how you are analyzing the text. Some of the things you might be doing are visualizing, asking questions, comparing, connecting the text to your own experience, or predicting. When you switch from reading to thinking aloud, be sure to give students a cue, either verbal or visual, that you're switching. When you have modeled this process several times, have students try it themselves with a partner. Encourage students to think aloud often, and continue to model the process for them regularly.

Fluency

Like thinking aloud, building fluency requires practice. Fluency is the ability to read at a smooth pace and with expression. Struggling readers often pause between words. They skip over punctuation, and they read very, very slowly. To achieve fluency, struggling readers must practice reading at every opportunity—reading, re-reading, reading aloud, reading along. In her book *When Kids Can't Read,* reading expert Kylene Beers notes, "Nonfluent readers are most often nonfluent because of lack of practice with reading" (218). Here are some ways to help students build fluency:

- To improve reading speed, work with students to master sight words and high-frequency words. Sight words are words readers need to know "on sight" because the words don't follow normal decoding rules. High-frequency words are words that are very common to a variety of texts. Encourage students to create their own word banks or flashcards, and practice with them until recognizing these words becomes automatic.

- Let students hear the texts they are reading. Read aloud to the class, modeling appropriate expression, phrasing and pacing. Invite students to read aloud individually or in choral readings.

- Teach students how to read aloud. Point out how internal punctuation affects the phrasing of a sentence and how end punctuation affects inflection. You can perform simple experiments with the class by adding, changing, or taking away punctuation from the same sentence.

- Have students re-read a text aloud several times. Once students have read and understood a passage, they can turn their attention to working on phrasing and pacing in subsequent readings.

- Don't immediately supply the correct word. When a student pauses over a word, give him or her time to figure it out. If the student continues to struggle, offer some ways of figuring out the word—looking for word parts, sounding it out, guessing what word would make sense in the context.

For more about these strategies and many others, you may want to look at the suggested readings that follow.

Suggested Readings

Beers, K. (2003). *When Kids Can't Read.* Portsmatter, NH: Heinemann.

Blevins, W. (2001). *Teaching Phonics and Word Study in the Intermediate Grades.* New York: Scholastic.

Browne, H., and Cambourne, B. (1990). *Read and Retell.* Portsmouth, NH: Heinemann.

Collins, C., and Pressley, M. (2002). *Comprehension Instruction: Research-Based Best Practices.* New York, NY: The Guilford Press.

Davey, B. (1983). "Think-Aloud: Modeling the Cognitive Processes of Reading Comprehension." *Journal of Reading, 27,* pp. 44–47.

Fischer, P., (1993). *The Sounds and Spelling Patterns of English: Phonics for Teachers and Parents.* Morrill, ME: Oxton House Publishers.

Harris, A. J., and Sipay, E. R. (1990). *How to Increase Reading Ability: A Guide to Developmental and Remedial Methods,* 8th edition. White Plains, NY: Longman.

Harvey, S., and Goudvis, A. (2000). *Strategies That Work: Teaching Comprehension to Enhance Understanding.* York, ME: Stenhouse Publishers.

Wilhelm, J. (2001). *Improving Comprehension with Think-Aloud Strategies.* New York, NY: Scholastic Professional Books.

Reading, Literary, and Vocabulary Skills

The lists on the following pages show the reading, literary, and vocabulary skills taught in each course of *Holt Adapted Reader*.

Third Course

Reading Skills

Literary Skills

Vocabulary Skills

Fourth Course

Reading Skills

Literary Skills

Vocabulary Skills

Fifth Course

Reading Skills

Literary Skills

Vocabulary Skills

Sixth Course

Reading Skills

Vocabulary Skills

Literary Skills

Pronunciation Guide

This chart will help you understand the phonetic spelling system used in *Holt Adapted Reader*. Look at this chart when you come to the phonetic spelling of a word you do not know. Find the symbol in the left-hand column that matches the symbol in the phonetic spelling. Then, look in the middle column. There you will find an example of the sound the symbol represents.

symbol(s)	example spelled normally	phonetic spelling
a	cat	(kat)
ay	pail	(payl)
ah	lot	(laht)
eh	hen	(hehn)
ee	me	(mee)
ih	willful	(WIHL fuhl)
y	buy	(by)
oh	grow	(groh)
aw	ball	(bawl)
u	book	(buk)
oo	new	(noo)
oy	boil	(boyl)
ow	house	(hows)
uh	ago, major, lawful	(uh GOH) (MAY juhr) (LAH fuhl)
ch	chalk	(chahk)
sh	show	(shoh)
th	thin	(thihn)
th	there	(*th*ehr)
zh	treasure	(TREH zhur)
ng	sing	(sihng)
l	metal	(MEH tl)
n	sudden	(SUH dn)
f	phone	(fohn)
k	can	(kan)
s	certain	(SUR tuhn)
g	get	(geht)
j	germ	(jurm)

Primary stress (**PRY** mayr ee)
Secondary stress (SEHK uhn DAYR ee)

Third Course

Answers to Annotations and Graphic Organizers

Far-out Housekeeping on the ISS Page 2

Page 4
Researching Questions
Circle "Listen to this story."

Page 5
Researching Questions
Sample response: I would expect to learn more about mission STS-106, as well as the space shuttle *Atlantis*.

Page 6
Researching Questions
Check "International Space Station."

Page 7
Graphic Organizer: Researching Questions

1. Answer provided.
2. c
3. b
4. d
5. a
6. e

A Christmas Memory Page 8

Page 10
Reading for Details
The details could appeal to the senses of taste, smell, sight, and touch.

Page 11
Reading for Details
Underline "rolled as tightly as spring buds" (sight, touch), "fifty-cent pieces heavy enough to weight a dead man's eyes" (touch), "the coin that really jingles" (hearing), "nickels and quarters worn smooth as creek pebbles" (touch), and "bitter-smelling pennies" (smell).

Setting
Underline "a large log cabin with chains of naked light bulbs hanging around it," "by the river's muddy edge," "At night, people have been murdered in Haha's," and "During the day, it is shabby and empty." Sample moods: scary, uncomfortable, creepy.

Page 12
Reading for Details
Circle "The black stove glows like a lighted pumpkin" (sight, touch), "Eggbeaters whirl" (hearing, sight), "spoons spin in bowls of butter and sugar" (sight, taste), "vanilla sweetens the air" (smell), "ginger spices it" (smell), "Melting, nose-tingling odors" (smell), "puffs of chimney smoke" (sight, smell), "Thirty-one cakes, damp with whiskey" (sight, smell, taste).

Reading for Details
The writer's friend is shy and does not make friends easily, but she appreciates and feels a bond with people who have been kind to her or who have done worthy deeds.

Reading for Details
Possible responses: Yes, the relatives were reasonable. It is unhealthy and dangerous to give whiskey to children. The writer and his friend are very drunk, dancing and singing loudly. No, the relatives overreacted. No harm was done, and the friends were having a good time. I think the writer would agree with this second position, because he makes the relatives sound cold and mean.

Page 13
Setting
Underline "Frost shines in the grass," "The sun makes the silvered winter woods shine," "A wild turkey calls," "a hog grunts in the undergrowth," "Our clothes catch on thorns, burs, and briers," "The path unwinds through lemony sun pools," and "inhales the pine-heavy air." The mood is happy, joyous, delightful. The two friends are having a wonderful day.

Page 14
Setting
The mood is contented or happy. Circle "Content," "sun-warmed," "peel oranges," "watch the kites in the sky."

Reading for Details
The mood of the ending is sad. The friends are separated and never see each other again.

Page 15
Graphic Organizer: Reading for Details
1. **Senses:** touch, sight. **Mood:** comfy.
2. **Senses:** sight, touch, hearing, taste, smell. **Mood:** happy.
3. **Senses:** touch, sight, hearing, smell. **Mood:** joyous.
4. Answer provided.

Teaching Chess, and Life / Feeding Frenzy Page 16

Page 18
Using Sources
Student responses will vary.

Using Sources
Chia had a positive and helpful impact on Carlos's life.

Page 19
Using Sources
Circle "think he's a good Samaritan."

Using Sources
Student answers will vary.

Page 20

Using Sources
Sample main idea: A young person was able to make the world a better place.

Page 21

Graphic Organizer: Using Sources
1. Primary
2. Secondary
3. Answer provided.
4. Primary
5. Secondary
6. Secondary

Marigolds   Page 22

Page 24

External and Internal Conflict
Circle "poverty."

Page 25

Making Inferences About Motivation
Underline "fear," "a hundred years old," "no sign of joy or pain," "she didn't like trespassers, especially children," "nobody ever visited her," "a witch," and "old fears." Sample answer: They pick on her because she is different and unfriendly. They are afraid of her and do not understand her.

Page 26

Making Inferences About Motivation
Lizabeth changes her mind when someone accuses her of being scared.

External and Internal Conflict
The battle between the children and Miss Lottie is an external conflict.

Page 27

External and Internal Conflict
The narrator's internal conflict is caused by growing up. She still is a child who finds the battle fun, but she is developing an adult sympathy for Miss Lottie and feels ashamed.

Vocabulary
Flinched means "drew back; winced."

Making Inferences About Motivation
Sample answer: Lizabeth looks up to her parents as sources of strength and safety. When her father cries, she no longer feels protected.

Page 28

External and Internal Conflict
Underline "lost my mind," "emotions swelled up in me," "need for my mother," "hopelessness of our poverty," "confusion of being neither child nor woman," "fear caused by my father's tears." Lizabeth expresses her internal conflict through external aggression—she destroys Miss Lottie's garden.

Making Inferences About Motivation
Lizabeth finally recognizes Miss Lottie as a fellow human being—a woman who is old, sad, and broken, yet who tries to find some beauty in life.

Page 29

Graphic Organizer: External and Internal Conflict
1. Answer provided.
2. Lizabeth wants to play with Joey and the other children, but she is starting to outgrow their kinds of games.
3. Lizabeth has an internal conflict about becoming a woman. She still wants to be a child and doesn't understand her new, more mature feelings.
4. The marigolds symbolize beauty found in a harsh world. Lizabeth first destroys them as an expression of her confusion and internal conflicts. At the end of the story, she says she has planted marigolds herself.

The Interlopers   Page 30

Page 32

Monitoring Your Reading
Ulrich thinks Georg and his men are disturbing the animals. Most students will probably agree. Some may think it is a dangerous predator.

Page 33

Monitoring Your Reading
Sample answer: Since line 69 says "the old hatred seemed to be dying," I predict his plan has something to do with ending the feud.

Page 34

Vocabulary
Underline "none other to interfere" and "from outside." *Interlopers* means "people who interfere in other people's affairs."

Surprise Ending
Sample answers: The surprise ending shows that Saki's message is: Being enemies can get you killed. Or, life is sometimes filled with nasty surprises.

Page 35

Graphic Organizer: Surprise Ending
Sample answers:
Explain: Answer provided.
Guess: The men are eaten by the wolves.
Analyze: The tragic surprise ending points out the danger of hating your neighbor.

The Necklace   Page 36

Page 39

Point of View
Circle "sad," "moody," and "upset."

Summarizing

Mathilde overcomes her difficulty by borrowing a diamond necklace from her friend.

Page 40

Summarizing

Mathilde's husband borrows the money.

Point of View

The lines reveal that Mme. Loisel has aged and lost her beauty but wishes she were still beautiful. Underline "remember when she had been so beautiful and admired" and "What if she hadn't lost the necklace? Who knows? How little there is between joy and misery!"

Page 41

Point of View

Underline "Mine was fake." This new information might change Mathilde's pride in her sacrifices to despair that she has suffered so much needlessly.

Page 42

Graphic Organizer: Third-Person-Limited Point of View

a. Answer provided.

b. Mathilde has married a middle-class civil servant.

c. She is unhappy because she is not rich and has no beautiful clothes.

d. She thinks she will be happy if she can dress well and be admired.

Graphic Organizer: Summarizing

Sample answers:

Somebody (Mathilde)

1. **wants** to go the party, **but** she doesn't have a nice enough gown, **so** her husband gives her the money.

2. **wants** beautiful jewelry to go with her gown, **but** she doesn't have any, **so** she borrows some from a friend.

Somebody (Mathilde's husband)

3. **wants** (answer provided), **but** Mathilde needs the money for a gown, **so** he gives her the money.

4. **wants** to replace the lost necklace, **but** he doesn't have enough money, **so** he borrows a great deal.

The Cask of Amontillado Page 44

Page 46

Vocabulary

Plotted means here "planned secretly."

Page 47

Unreliable Narrator

- The narrator mentions a concern for Fortunato's health to fool Fortunato into thinking the narrator is his friend.

- He mentions Luchesi to make Fortunato jealous and anxious to taste the amontillado himself.

Page 48

Drawing Conclusions

Sample responses: The narrator is cruel. He holds a deep grudge. He hates Fortunato so much that he is happy to hear him moan.

Unreliable Narrator

Sample response: He is covering up his true feelings. What he's doing is so monstrous that it is making him physically ill. Underline "My heart grew sick" and "May he rest in peace."

Page 49

Graphic Organizer: Unreliable Narrator

Sample responses:

1. No—He says he was insulted by Fortunato, but no one else seems to have noticed. Also he seems to be very wealthy. Insane.

2. Answer provided.

3. Yes—When Montresor keeps pretending he will go to Luchesi, Fortunato's pride in his superior understanding of wines keeps him following Montresor down to the catacombs. Sane.

4. Yes—He has made sure the servants have left the palace. He has bought mason's tools to build a wall. He has stored stones and cement at the location of the new wall. He has created a story to lure Fortunato to his death. Sane.

5. Pleased—He listened "with satisfaction" to Fortunato's moans. He mimics Fortunato's screams. Insane.

Guilty or Not Guilty? Answers will vary.

Poe's Death Is Rewritten as Case of Rabies, Not Telltale Alcohol / If Only Poe Had Succeeded When He Said Nevermore to Drink / Rabies Death Theory Page 50

Page 52

Synthesizing Sources

Underline "Poe was confused, angry, and aggressive," "it was difficult for him to drink water," "rabies victims often don't remember being bitten," "Once the signs appear, patients die in a few days," "Poe's doctor may have changed the details of Poe's death," "a glass of wine made him ill for days," "Poe almost always avoided alcohol."

Page 53

Synthesizing Sources

Underline "Dr. Benitez is wrong to say that rabies, not alcoholism, caused Poe's death."

Synthesizing Sources

Circle "Poe was found drunk and unconscious outside a bar," "Four people who saw Poe . . . agree that Poe was drunk," "Poe wrote often about his periods of heavy drinking," "rabies symptoms were easily recognized," "Poe's pet cat, Caterina, showed no sign of rabies."

Synthesizing Sources

The main ideas in the article and letter are the opposite. The article says Poe died of rabies, not alcohol. The letter says Poe died of alcoholism, not rabies.

Page 54

Synthesizing Sources

Student responses will vary.

Page 55

Graphic Organizer: Synthesizing Sources

1. **a.** Poe died of rabies, not alcohol.
   b. Poe died of alcoholism, not rabies.
   c. Answer provided.
2. **a.** All of Poe's symptoms point to rabies.
   b. Witnesses said Poe was drunk.
   c. Answer provided.
3. **a., b., c.** The article and first letter have opposite points of view. The second letter supports the article.
4. **a.** Answer provided.
   b., c. Student answers will vary.

Sample synthesis statement: Scholars continue to disagree about what caused Poe's death.

A Country Divided / Lives in the Crossfire   Page 56

Page 58

Synthesizing Sources

This is a secondary source. You can tell because it uses the third person and describes events the writer did not participate in.

Page 59

Vocabulary

Circle "fought with words," "regained the vote," and "change the laws."

Synthesizing Sources

The passage contains just facts. All the sentences could be underlined as evidence.

Page 60

Synthesizing Sources

Possible sources: encyclopedias, Internet searches, newspaper articles, books.

Page 61

Synthesizing Sources

The text is a secondary source.

Page 62

Synthesizing Sources

• **Purpose:** to teach about the effect of the Troubles on the daily life and on children in Northern Ireland.
• **Audience:** young people, anyone interested in the Troubles in Ireland.

Page 63

Graphic Organizer: Synthesizing Sources

1. **b.** Answer provided.
   c. To inform. To elicit sympathy for the suffering in Northern Ireland.
2. **b.** Anyone interested in Irish history.
   c. Young people, anyone concerned about the problems in Ireland.
3. **b.** Answer provided.
   c. A combination of historical facts and the author's thoughts and feelings.

The Gift of the Magi   Page 64

Page 66

Making Predictions

Sample answer: She is thinking about doing something with her hair—maybe cutting or selling it. Underline "she pulled down her hair."

Page 67

Vocabulary

Collected means here "regained control of."

Making Predictions

Students' expectations will vary. Possible response: He seems stunned because he was used to her hair and loved it.

Page 68

Making Predictions

Some students may figure out that since Della sold her hair to buy his watch fob, Jim will have sold his watch to buy her combs.

Situational Irony

Circle "I sold the watch to get the money to buy your combs."

Page 69

Graphic Organizer: Situational Irony

1. Answer provided.
2. It would have been the perfect gift, but Jim sold the watch to buy her present.
3. Della loves the combs, but she sold her hair to buy Jim's gift.

The Lady, or the Tiger?   Page 70

Page 72

Vocabulary

Fancy means here "whim, desire, or inclination."

Page 73

Making Inferences About Motivation

Sample answer: The king created this system of justice because it amuses him and he likes to have his own way.

Making Inferences About Motivation
Underline "handsome," "brave," and "fine." Circle "Never before had a commoner dared to love the daughter of a king."

Making Inferences About Motivation
The king has the trial because it amuses him and gives him pleasure. He enjoys the drama, whatever happens.

Page 74

Making Inferences About Motivation
Possible responses: The princess comes to the trial to see what happens or to influence the outcome.

Making Inferences About Motivation
Possible responses: The lover follows the princess's signal because he loves and trusts her or because he wants to let her choose his fate.

Ambiguity
Answers will vary.

Page 75

Graphic Organizer: Ambiguity Chart
The Lady: The princess loves the young man passionately.
The Tiger: Answer provided. Add: The princess has a passionate and headstrong nature.
My decision: Sample answers—The tiger comes out because the princess has a passionate nature and would rather her lover die than be with another woman. The lady comes out because the princess loves the young man so much she couldn't bear to see him die.

A Defense of the Jury System Page 76

Page 78

Evaluating an Argument
Underline "they would rather be tried by their peers than by a panel of judges," "jurors do at least 'moderately well,'" and "they would rather have their case decided by a jury instead of a judge."

Evaluating an Argument
Underline "judges, like jurors, are human beings who can make mistakes"; "judges do not represent society"; "A jury reflects different backgrounds and points of view."

Evaluating an Argument
Sample answer: The jury system is not perfect, but it's the best we've got.

Page 79

Graphic Organizer: Evaluating an Argument
1. d
2. Answer provided.
3. a
4. c
5. e

Letter to President Roosevelt Page 80

Page 82

Connecting
Students may know that German aggression was the cause of World War II and that the United States eventually joined Great Britain and the Soviet Union in fighting against Germany, Italy, and Japan.

Page 83

Graphic Organizer: Paraphrasing and Connecting
Paraphrase: Soon a nuclear chain reaction will probably be set off in a large amount of uranium. Huge power and lots of radiation will be created. It might be possible to use this to build a new kind of bomb. Even one of these bombs would destroy a large area, but such a bomb would be too heavy to carry in a plane.

There is not much good uranium in the United States, but there is in Canada, Czechoslovakia, and the Belgian Congo.

You should get government officials to contact the scientists working on this. Choose someone trustworthy to keep people informed, to find more uranium, and to raise money.

Germany no longer sells uranium from Czechoslovakia. This may be because the Germans are doing similar research with uranium.
Connect: Students may have some knowledge of World War II, Germany, Nazis, nuclear war, Hiroshima, and Nagasaki, for example.
Respond: Answers will vary.

The Seven Ages of Man Page 84

Page 86

Paraphrasing a Poem
Sample answer: Old age is like the last scene in a play. This is when a person's strange and eventful life comes to an end. This is a person's second childhood. At this age in life, the person forgets everything, doesn't have any teeth, can't see, can't taste, and has lost everything.

Page 88

Graphic Organizer: Extended Metaphor
Sample answers:
One—Answer provided.
Two—**Your Ages:** 5–18. **Your Roles:** Student, son or daughter, brother or sister.
Three—**Your Ages:** 19–22. **Your Roles:** College student, worker, boyfriend or girlfriend.
Four—**Your Ages:** 22–40. **Your Roles:** Worker, such as teacher, soldier, artist, lawyer, etc; husband or wife; parent.
Five—**Your Ages:** 40–65. **Your Roles:** Same as above but more established and successful, parent, grandparent.
Six—**Your Ages:** 65–80. **Your Roles:** Retiree, community volunteer, grandparent.
Seven—**Your Ages:** 80–100. **Your Roles:** Person in a retirement community or nursing home.

Page 89

Graphic Organizer: Paraphrasing

Sample answers:
1. The world's like a stage and people are actors. They are born and die. In between, they go through seven stages.
2. The student carries his book bag. He has a clean face in the morning and goes slowly and reluctantly to school.
3. The soldier swears a lot and has a rough beard. He is quick to fight over his honor and seeks fame in battle.

I Wandered Lonely as a Cloud Page 90

Page 93

Reading a Poem

Students may appreciate the effects of the stanza's sound when they read it aloud.

Rhythm and Meter

And dánces with the dáffodils.

Page 94

Graphic Organizer: Reading a Poem

Stanza 1: Answers provided.
Stanza 2: Slashes after "bay;" and "dance." Circle "They" and "I." Underline "stretched" and "saw."
Stanza 3: Slashes after "glee;" "company;" and "brought." Circle "waves," "they," "poet," and "I." Underline "danced," "outdid," "be," "gazed—and gazed," and "thought."
Stanza 4: Slashes after "mood," "solitude;" and "daffodils." Circle "I," "They," and "heart." Underline "lie," "flash," "fills," and "dances."
The poem makes me feel—Sample responses: happy, joyous, peaceful.

Page 95

Vocabulary Development: Developing Vocabulary

1. pensive. Sample sentence: In the library, people often have a pensive look.
2. Answers provided.
3. solitude. Sample sentence: There is a spot by the lake I go to when I want solitude.
4. jocund. Sample sentence: The jocund class laughed at the funny events in the story.

Rising Tides Page 96

Page 98

Evaluating an Argument

Underline "seasons are changing," "Rainstorms are becoming more intense," "Sea levels are rising," "glaciers are shrinking," "permafrost . . . is thawing," "Trees are flowering earlier," and "Insects are coming out sooner."

Evaluating an Argument

Circle "A report by the Intergovernmental Panel on Climate Change."

Page 99

Evaluating an Argument

Underline "Carbon dioxide . . . stays in the atmosphere for more than a hundred years. The effects of our failure to act will last for centuries."

Evaluating an Argument

Circle "ignore," "feasting greedily," and "hurting the planet." Sample explanation: Herbert makes this emotional appeal because he is very concerned about the environment and wants to convince his audience to take action to save it.

Page 100

Graphic Organizer: Evaluating an Argument

Sample answers:
Claim: The United States should do something to end global warming now.
Logical Appeals: Reason 1: Answer provided.
Evidence: Answer provided.
Reason 2: People most responsible for global warming will be least hurt by it. **Evidence:** Industrial nations pollute most but also have money, technology, and so on to cope with problems of global warming. Poor countries do not.
Reason 3: The United States has a special responsibility.
Evidence: The United States is the strongest, most polluting nation, so we should sacrifice to be fair to neighbors.
Emotional Appeals: Loaded words: "pretend," "vanish," "scary rate," "astonished," "strange," "disaster," "harmed," "more than a hundred years," "responsibility," "mightiest," "fair," "sacrifices," "feasting greedily."

Page 101

Vocabulary Development: Loaded Words

1. **Sample response:** I think of fun, playing games, and playacting. There is also a bad side—pretending to be something you are not.
   Sample sentence: When I was little, I liked to pretend I was Spider-Man.
2. **Sample response:** I think of horror movies and of people fighting wars.
   Sample sentence: The haunted house at the amusement park isn't very scary.
3. Answers provided.
4. **Sample response:** I feel proud thinking of my country or of my favorite team.
   Sample sentence: Our school team was the mightiest in the league.

American History Page 102

Page 104

Biographical Approach
Underline "My dreams were about going to college and becoming a teacher."

Historical Approach
Underline "the day that President Kennedy was shot."

Page 105

Historical Approach
Underline "His voice broke, and he covered his face with his hands"; "No one moved for a minute; then we all scrambled madly to get out of there"; "a profound silence"; and "tear-streaked face."
Possible answer: The adults in the story are very sad when President Kennedy is killed. The children are confused and don't know what to think.

Biographical Approach
Possible response: Her mother means that Elena will suffer the humiliation and pain of prejudice or rejection.

Page 106

Summarizing
Sample answer: Elena knocks and Eugene's mother answers the door. She asks if Elena lives in El Building. When Elena says yes, the mother tells her that Eugene can't study with her. She tells Elena to go away. At home in bed, Elena tries to think of the dead president, but she is really crying for herself.

Page 107

Graphic Organizer: Summarizing
Sample answers:
Event 1: Answer provided.
Event 2: Elena meets and becomes friends with Eugene.
Event 3: Answer provided.
Event 4: The students are sent home from school.
Event 5: Answer provided.
Event 6: Eugene's mother won't let Elena study with Eugene.

From the Odyssey, Part One Page 108

Page 110

Monitor Your Comprehension
The Cyclops closed the cave with a huge slab of rock.

Page 111

Vocabulary
Underline "cast your lives like dice, and ravage other folk."

Vocabulary
Ravage means "destroy; ruin."

Page 114

Vocabulary
Din means "loud noise."

Heroes
Odysseus's plan is to sharpen a tree trunk into a point and, with his men's help, thrust it into the Cyclops's eye. The plan is heroic because it is difficult and dangerous. It requires great strength and daring.

Page 115

Vocabulary
Nectar and ambrosia are what the gods drink and eat, so the Cyclops means the wine is very delicious.

Page 116

Monitor Your Comprehension
Possible response: Odysseus doesn't want the Cyclops to know his real name.

Monitor Your Comprehension
Odysseus and his men thrust the red-hot stake into the Cyclops's eye.

Page 117

Monitor Your Comprehension
Underline "bellowed"; "Clawing his face he tugged the bloody spike out of his eye, threw it away"; "went groping"; "set up a howl."

Page 118

Vocabulary
Sage means "wise."

Heroes
Odysseus ties each man under the middle ram of three rams, which are tied together. He then holds himself under the biggest, woolliest ram and waits till morning.

Page 119

Monitor Your Comprehension
Students may connect to affectionate feelings for a pet, sibling, or friend.

Page 120

Vocabulary
Adversary means "opponent."

Heroes
He gives orders to hurry and load the herd onto the ship.

Page 121

Heroes
Sample answers: Yes, because he shows great bravery and pride. No, because his anger and pride put him and his men in danger.

Page 122

Monitor Your Comprehension
Polyphemus has expected a giant for an adversary, so he is surprised that someone as small and pitiful as Odysseus could defeat him.

Monitor Your Comprehension
The Cyclops offers to treat Odysseus well and pray to his father, Poseidon, to help him if he returns. Sample response: No, I think he really wants to kill Odysseus.

Page 123

Monitor Your Comprehension
Odysseus's taunting results in the Cyclops praying to Poseidon to grant that Odysseus never sees his home, or at least not for many years, and that he have hard times and lose all his men and return to bad days at home. Most students will predict that Odysseus's journey will be full of grief.

Page 124

Graphic Organizer: Heroes
For Odysseus, check the following characteristics: Attractive, Proud, Adventurous, Helpful, Has enemies, and Clever. Heroic characteristics of students' heroes will vary.

Page 125

Vocabulary Development: Synonyms
1. Answer provided.
2. h
3. i
4. f
5. a
6. g
7. c
8. j
9. b
10. d

From the Odyssey, Part Two Page 126

Page 128

Vocabulary
Snuffling means "sniffing or sniffling." Underline "the dogs," "belly down," and "not one has even growled."

Page 129

Living Characters
Sample answer: I like and trust a person who speaks honestly.

Page 130

Vocabulary
Telemachus stopped Odysseus from moving from the couch.

Living Characters
Telemachus's behavior shows that he is polite and courteous to strangers.

Page 131

Living Characters
Circle "noble" and "enduring."

Monitor Your Comprehension
Sample answers: I'd probably feel weird and back away. I'd be thrilled to finally meet my father.

Page 132

Living Characters
Underline "Odysseus brought his ranging mind to bear" (line 90) and "So helplessly they cried, pouring out tears,/and might have gone on weeping so till sundown" (lines 104–105).
Sample response: Odysseus acts like a hero when he wisely answers his son and like an ordinary father when he hugs his son and cries.

Page 133

Living Characters
Antinous is young, rich, unaware of danger, and having a good time among his friends.

Page 134

Monitor Your Comprehension
Sample answer: The other suitors jump up and look for their arms, which aren't there, and then they threaten Odysseus. Based on the words "they were already in the grip of death," I predict Odysseus will kill them.

Page 135

Vocabulary
Odysseus has an angry look on his face.

Living Characters
Sample response: It is cowardly to blame someone else for your actions, but since Antinous is already dead and Eurymachus and his friends have no weapons, it may be a wise thing to say.

Page 136

Monitor Your Comprehension
Underline "we'll make/restitution of wine and meat consumed/and add, each one, a tithe of twenty oxen/ with gifts of bronze and gold." Sample answers: Odysseus is too angry to take the offer. He thinks their faults are too great to be forgiven.

Monitor Your Comprehension
Sample answers: I'd be scared. I'd be excited.

Page 137

Monitor Your Comprehension
Sample answers:
Lines 70–73: The comparison of the suitors to cattle stampeding because of gadflies makes the scene feel very chaotic, crazy, and maybe a bit silly.
Lines 74–79: The comparison of the attackers to falcons diving down on flights of birds makes the scene feel violent and scary, yet majestic.

Page 138

Living Characters
Underline "she, for a long time, sat deathly still in wonderment." Sample answer: Penelope's reaction shows that she hasn't seen her husband in so long that she is not sure she recognizes him. It also shows that she is careful and takes her time in making up her mind.

Page 139

Living Characters

Circle "patient hero" and "Greathearted." Sample answer: Athena makes Odysseus look handsome, tall, and big, with red curly hair.

Page 140

Vocabulary

Aloof means "distant."

Living Characters

Sample answers: He is running out of patience. He wants to goad Penelope into responding.

Page 141

Monitor Your Comprehension

Sample answer: One bed post is made from a trunk of an olive tree growing in the ground. The other posts look like it. The posts are inlaid with silver, gold, and ivory. A web of red leather strips form the bed.

Page 142

Monitor Your Comprehension

Sample responses: Yes, it is fitting to have a joyful reunion to end Odysseus's long years of suffering. No, a reunion is too tame and domestic a scene to end such heroic adventures.

Page 143

Graphic Organizer: Living Characters

1. **Odysseus:** Answer provided. **Telemachus:** "Friend, sit down; we'll find another chair in our own hut." **Penelope:** "You make my stiff heart know that I am yours."
2. **Odysseus:** He weeps with his son. He kills all the suitors. **Telemachus:** Answer provided. **Penelope:** She tests Odysseus to be sure who he is.
3. **Odysseus:** Penelope says, "No one ever matched your caution!" **Telemachus:** The swineherd says, "Light of my days, Telemachus." **Penelope:** Answer provided.
4. **Odysseus:** Answer provided. **Telemachus:** The narrator describes him as young and honest, with shining eyes. **Penelope:** The narrator describes her as a dear wife, clear and faithful.

Heroes with Solid Feet Page 144

Page 146

Evaluating an Argument

Underline "It's better to look for little heroes, and to try to be one."

Page 147

Graphic Organizer: Evaluating an Argument

Sample answers:
Author's Intent: Answer provided.

Support for Argument: Check "Emotional appeal" box. A Jewish women in Berlin tells about how she was saved by ordinary Germans—"the little heroes"—who hid her during the war.
Author's Tone: Serious.

The Tragedy of Romeo and Juliet, Act II, Scene 2 Page 148

Page 151

Figures of Speech

Circle "bright angel."

Page 152

Connecting with the Text

Some students may say new lovers today might act in a similar way—Juliet is mostly asking, "Who is this?" Romeo is expressing his love is a lively, bantering way. Other students may think lovers today would be more direct and open or less direct and open.

Page 154

Figures of Speech

Underline "did prompt me," "He lent me counsel," and "I lent him eyes."

Connecting with the Text

Sample response: A teenage girl today definitely would feel embarrassed if the guy she liked overheard her talking about him!

Page 155

Figures of Speech

The "god" Juliet is referring to is Romeo.

Vocabulary

Rash means here "hasty."

Page 156

Figures of Speech

Circle "My bounty is as boundless as the sea." The figure of speech is a simile. I know because it uses the word *as.*

Page 157

Vocabulary

Substantial means here "real."

Page 158

Figures of Speech

Sample answer: When a person is waiting anxiously for something, the wait always seems much longer.

Connecting with the Text

Most students will have had a similar experience. Sample response: Juliet doesn't want Romeo to go, so she doesn't really need another reason to call him back.

Page 159

Connecting with the Text

Sample response: The sound of the alliteration makes the phrase fun to say. The combination "sweet sorrow" is surprising but realistically reflects how some kinds of sorrow feel.

Page 160

Graphic Organizer: Figures of Speech

Sample answers:
1. Answer provided.
2. The beginning of their love is young and new, but with time it will grow into a beautiful relationship.
3. Juliet's ability to give has no boundaries, and her love is as deep as the sea. The more she gives to Romeo, the more she will have.
4. Romeo says that he is as sad to go away from Juliet as it is for a schoolboy to go toward school.

Page 161

Vocabulary Development: Developing Vocabulary

Sample answers:
1. Jeannette has a perverse reaction that makes her want to do the opposite of what anyone asks.
2. Everyone asked his plans, but Andre kept his own counsel.
3. The philanthropist was known for his bounty to local charities.

The Tragedy of Romeo and Juliet, Act III, Scene 5 Page 162

Page 165

Paraphrasing

Sample response: Go—the sun is rising. The more time that passes, the worse our problems become.

Page 166

Paraphrasing

Sample response: Write to me often, for every minute away from you seems like days. So it will seem like years until I see you again.

Page 167

Dramatic Irony

We know that Juliet is weeping over Romeo's banishment.

Page 168

Vocabulary

Want means here "lack."

Dramatic Irony

Juliet is really talking about Romeo.

Page 169

Dramatic Irony

Juliet really means that she won't be satisfied till she sees Romeo. The word *dead* goes with the next line to mean that her heart is dead toward her cousin.

Page 170

Dramatic Irony

The reader knows that Juliet is already married to Romeo.

Page 171

Paraphrasing

Sample answer: Yes, sir, but though she thanks you, she won't do it. She is such a fool; I wish she were dead!

Page 172

Vocabulary

Underline "a sled that transports criminals to be executed."

Paraphrasing

Sample answer: Dear father, I'm begging you to give me a chance to talk.

Dramatic Irony

It shows dramatic irony because Juliet will soon be dead and unable to look her father in the face.

Page 173

Vocabulary

Gravity means here "matter of importance."

Page 174

Vocabulary

Monument means here "tomb."

Paraphrasing

Sample answer: Don't talk to me because I won't answer. Do whatever you want, I don't care.

Page 175

Dramatic Irony

It is ironic because Romeo will soon be dead.

Page 176

Vocabulary

Circle "wicked" or "damnation."

Page 177

Graphic Organizer: Paraphrasing

Sample answers:
1. Are you still crying over your cousin? Are you trying to wash him out of his grave with tears?
2. Oh, how I hate to hear Romeo's name mentioned without being able to be with him.
3. Answer provided.
4. Oh, misery, that heaven should try to trick such a weak person as me.

The Tragedy of Romeo and Juliet, Act IV, Scene 3 Page 178

Page 180

Making Inferences

Juliet wants to be alone so she can drink the potion Friar Laurence gave her.

Page 181

Making Inferences

Juliet means she will kill herself with the dagger if the potion does not work.

Soliloquy

Circle "What if it be poison."

Page 182

Soliloquy

Possible response: Juliet is frightened and is getting more and more upset and hysterical.

Vocabulary

Spit means here "spear."

Page 183

Graphic Organizer: Soliloquy

Sample answers:
1. Answers provided.
2. **Summary:** What if I wake up in the tomb before Romeo comes to get me? **Juliet's State of Mind:** Juliet is becoming scared.
3. **Summary:** Look! I think I see Tybalt's ghost coming after Romeo who killed him. Stop, Tybalt! **Juliet's State of Mind:** Juliet is becoming hysterical.

Romeo and Juliet in Bosnia   Page 184

Page 186

Making Connections

Sample answer: Another similarity is that both pairs of lovers have relatives opposed to their relationship.

Making Connections

The writer says that the basis of the conflict in this story is the cause of all wars—ethnic or religious reasons.

Page 187

Graphic Organizer: Making Connections

Sample answers:
1. Answer provided.
2. **Connecting work:** *West Side Story* **Event:** Two lovers die in a gang fight.
3. **Connecting work:** "Lives in the Crossfire" **Event:** People's lives are disrupted by the conflict between the Catholics and the Protestants in Northern Ireland.

Fourth Course

Answers to Annotations and Graphic Organizers

Diary of a Mad Blender: A Week of Managing Every Spare Minute Page 2

Page 4
Identifying the Main Idea
The author feels drained by all her time management efforts. She also feels as though she's not spending enough time with her daughter.

Page 6
Graphic Organizer: Seeing the Big Picture

Supporting Evidence: The author has difficulty combining work and play when she takes her kids snowboarding.
Supporting Evidence: The author tries to cram in extra tasks while she's doing other things, but ends up feeling tense and rattled.
Supporting Evidence: The author attempts to do work while watching TV at the expense of not spending time with her daughter.
Main Idea: It's harder than it looks to juggle work and everything else. Cramming so many tasks into one's schedule leaves little time to rest or spend with family.

Page 7
Vocabulary Development: Analogies
1. Part of something to the whole.
2. Thing/object to the category it belongs to.
3. Thing to a characteristic of the thing.
4. Worker to a tool the worker uses.

A Baby's Quilt to Sew Up the Generations Page 8

Page 10
Understanding Secondary Sources
The main idea is that quilts serve as a way to link families together in the present while also serving as a bridge to the past. This idea is supported by the anecdotes in the article that tell how quilting has brought families closer together.

Page 11
Graphic Organizer: Source Quilt
Accept any sources that legitimately support the event the student chooses.

By Any Other Name Page 12

Page 14
Vocabulary
Clues include "two names" and "split personality."

Comparison and Contrast
The Indian girls sit at the back of the class, which implies that they are treated as second-class citizens. The Indian girls also wear some traditional clothing (though one girl is wearing a dress like those the English girls wear).

Page 15
Character and Autobiography
Premila is much more aware of the fact that she and her sister are different from the other girls. She's embarrassed by the fact that they stand out.

Page 16
Comparison and Contrast
Santha is too young to be embarrassed by the fact that she and Premila are different from the other girls at school. Premila, however, wants to try to fit in by bringing sandwiches for lunch instead of Indian food.

Vocabulary
Clues include the word "suddenly" and the fact that Premila removes Santha from school in the middle of the day.

Character and Autobiography
Premila has a clear sense of right and wrong. She recognizes that she and her sister are being treated unfairly because they are Indian, so she takes action.

Page 18
Graphic Organizer: Characterization
Sample responses follow.
1. Santha wants to wear cotton dresses to school instead of traditional Indian clothes. This shows that she wants to fit in with the other girls. This is indirect characterization.
2. Santha seems unconcerned that she's eating Indian food for lunch. This shows that she has limited awareness of what makes her different from the other girls. This is indirect characterization.
3. Santha doesn't understand the concept of winning when she plays games with the other children during recess. This doesn't seem to faze her, however. This is indirect characterization.
4. Even though Santha is young, she realizes that she can't be friends with the English children. This shows that she is aware of class distinctions to some extent. This is direct characterization.

Page 19
Vocabulary Development: Putting Words in Context
Answers will vary.

The Cold Equations Page 20

Page 22
Asking Questions
Sample response: Who is in the supply closet?

Page 23
Third-Person-Limited Point of View
The man seems to feel compassion for others.

Page 24
Third-Person-Limited Point of View
The narrator stays outside the action of the story.

Page 25

Third-Person-Limited Point of View
The tone is detached and objective.

Page 26

Vocabulary
Sample response: *Range* means "the limits." The ship won't be able to contact Gerry once his camp passes the limits of the signal.

Page 27

Asking Questions
Sample response: Why is Marilyn defending the pilot when she knows he's going to kill her?

Page 28

Vocabulary
Sample responses: The pilot brings the ship's weight into balance; the pilot balances Marilyn's life against the lives of the six sick men; the ship's temperature is brought back into balance.

Asking Questions
Sample responses: How will the pilot live with himself after this? How will he deal with his feelings of guilt? Wasn't there something else to try?

Page 29

Graphic Organizer: Analyzing Point of View
Sample responses are provided.
1. The narrator is someone who is outside the action of the story.
2. The narrator knows the inner thoughts of Barton, the main character.
3. The narrator does not know the inner thoughts of the girl.
4. Because we know more about Barton's thoughts and feelings, it's easier to sympathize with him.
5. The story could be told in the first person from the point of view of the girl. Then, we would know much less about Barton's character.

Taste—The Final Frontier Page 30

Page 32

Generating Research Questions
Sample responses: How would astronauts react when their diet is not varied enough? What changes in diet might bring about an improvement in the astronauts' well-being?

Page 33

Graphic Organizer: Research Question Chart
Sample responses are provided.
1. Answer provided.
2. What foods do astronauts like best? What happens if astronauts do not have a variety of food? What recipes provide the most variety for the food? What are some of the dietary restrictions and requirements of space travelers?

3. What plants best fulfill these requirements? What factors limit the variety of plants that can be grown in space?
4. What kinds of animals can survive in space? Of these animals, which ones can be used as a food source for astronauts? What kind of environment would be needed for animals in space?

Typhoid Fever Page 34

Page 36

Evaluating Credibility
Sample response: His response is credible because (1) because he is now a writer, he already might have been able to recognize great writing; and (2) he might actually remember his feelings at the time.

Page 37

Evaluating Credibility
Sample response: Her response does seem credible. Nurses are expected to enforce the rules, and that's what she's trying to do.

Page 38

Voice
Underlined words or word groups may include "Protestant soup any soup" and "howling for bits of my chocolate bar."

Vocabulary
Sample response: A *privilege* is a right or favor a person receives for good behavior.

Page 39

Graphic Organizer: Voice
Sample responses are provided.
1. Comic; McCourt references all the inside jokes he has with Patricia when they're both in the hospital.
2. Intelligent; McCourt talks about Shakespeare and "The Highwayman."

The Man in the Water Page 40

Page 42

Essay
Sample response: The author believes that anyone will risk his or her life to save another person's life. Accept any reasonable claim and its support.

Page 43

Graphic Organizer: Summarizing Main Idea
Sample responses are provided.

The park police on the helicopter team risked their lives picking up survivors.
The "man in the water" passed the lifeline on to other passengers.
The "man in the water" is an example that the rest of us can follow.

If Decency Doesn't, Law Should Make Us Samaritans / Good Samaritans U.S.A. Are Afraid to Act Page 44

Page 46

Evaluating Arguments

The authors are using an emotional appeal by mentioning the fact that any of the reader's loved ones could be in an accident and need help.

Page 47

Evaluating Arguments

The author does not think people should be required to be good Samaritans because they might run the risk of being sued if they cause unintentional harm to the person they try to help.

Page 48

Evaluating Arguments

The author makes the claim that lawyers can make it seem as though doctors have a "duty" to treat people in emergency situations.

Page 49

Graphic Organizer: Evaluating Arguments

Sample answers are provided.

If Decency Doesn't . . .

Writer's Opinion, or Claim: People should be required to help others so that needless deaths can be avoided.
Main Idea: There should be a good-Samaritan law requiring everyone to help others.
Supporting Evidence: Helping people could mean the difference between life and death.
Emotional Appeals: The person in need could be someone you love; "bleeding, injured, and dying"
Intent: The author wants to change readers' thinking about the issue of good-Samaritan laws.
Tone: Serious, persuasive.

Good Samaritans U.S.A. . . .

Writer's Opinion, or Claim: Americans don't help strangers because they fear being hurt or sued.
Main Idea: In our current social climate, people should not be required by law to help others.
Supporting Evidence: Some current good-Samaritan laws confuse the issue because they are subject to varying legal interpretations.
Emotional Appeals: None. The article relies mostly on logical appeals.
Intent: The author wants to point out the problems with good-Samaritan laws.
Tone: Logical, rational.

R.M.S. Titanic Page 50

Page 52

Vocabulary

Circled word: "chunks."

Page 53

Irony

The use of the pumps is an example of dramatic irony because we know the ship will sink.

Understanding Text Structures

Knowing the exact times helps the reader see how quickly events took place, and how little time the crew had to make decisions.

Page 54

Vocabulary

Underlined meaning: "small room."

Irony

It is situational irony.

Page 55

Irony

Sample response: It is situational irony because we did not expect the *Titanic* to sink on its first voyage.

Vocabulary

Underlined meaning: "put on duty." Sample explanation: The lookout was put on duty to see what was in the ship's path.

Page 56

Graphic Organizer: Dramatic and Situational Irony

Sample explanations are below.
1. D: This is dramatic irony because the audience knows ignoring this warning from the *Californian* will result in the destruction of the *Titanic*.
2. S: This is situational irony because I would not expect the band to play jolly music while the ship is sinking. In fact, I wouldn't think it would play at all.
3. S: This is situational irony because I would expect the lifeboats to be full to save as many people as possible.
4. Answer provided.

Page 57

Vocabulary Development: Words with More than One Meaning

Underlined meanings are listed below.
1. Answer provided
2. message sent by radio
3. front part of ship
4. training exercise

Into Thin Air Page 58

Page 60
Cause and Effect
Sample response: Krakauer had to climb down without oxygen because Andy Harris accidentally opened the valve of Krakauer's oxygen tank and let all the oxygen out.

Page 61
Cause and Effect
Underlined sentence: "None of them suspected that on that day, every minute would count."

Vocabulary
Sample response: "top."

Page 62
Cause and Effect
Sample response: Hall stayed with Hansen because he thought that all the bottles of oxygen waiting for them at South Summit were empty.

Vocabulary
Underlined words: "the local guides from Nepal."

Page 63
Cause and Effect
Underlined sentence: "Famous mountain climbers . . . have always been those who took great risks and got away with it."

Page 64
Graphic Organizer: Cause-and-Effect Chart
Sample responses are below.

Cause: Weathers decided to wait at 27,500 feet for Hall and the group to return.
Cause: Weathers refused to take Krakauer's advice and return with him.

Page 65
Vocabulary Development: Analogies and Comprehension
A.
1. summit
2. blizzard
3. vision
4. amputate
5. collapsed
6. descent
B.
Accept any original sentences correctly using the selected vocabulary words.

Vision Quest Page 66

Page 68
Analyzing an Encyclopedia Article
guardian spirit

Page 69
Graphic Organizer: Analyzing an Encyclopedia Article
Sample responses are below.
1. The main subject of the article is the vision quest.
2. The information about another article on a connected topic is given in a footnote at the bottom of the page.
3. Other related topics mentioned in the article are the tribes or groups that go on vision quests, vision quest rituals, and guardian animals. Accept any topic presented in the article.
4. Two vision-quest techniques are watching for an animal that behaves in a meaningful way or discovering an object that looks like some animal. Other techniques may include dreaming of an animal, going on a dream journey, and learning from the dream animal.
5. Answer provided.

The Masque of the Red Death
Page 70

Page 72
Asking Questions
Sample response: One cannot see from one room to another. Each room has its own color—blue, purple, green, orange, white, violet, and black—creating a carnival-like atmosphere. The last room is black and scary because of the blood-red light cast by a fire on the other side of the tall red windows.

Page 73
Asking Questions
Sample answer: The chiming of the clock makes the partygoers pause and become confused and anxious.

Vocabulary
"horror" and "disgust"

Allegory
Sample response: The new guest could represent death because the figure is compared to a corpse and is covered from head to foot.

Page 75
Asking Questions
Sample response: The guest is the Red Death. All the partygoers die.

Page 76
Graphic Organizer: Allegory
Sample responses follow.
1. *Prince Prospero:* Because his name sounds like "prosperous," he might represent wealth or success.
2. *the seven rooms:* The rooms and their arrangement may represent the stages of life because when you are in one stage of life, you can see only a little of the next stage ahead.
3. *the clock:* The passage of time.
4. *the uninvited guest:* The Red Death.

Vocabulary Development: Strategies for Using Context Clues

1. context clues: "deep chimes rang out"
   definition: "rang"
2. context clues: "horror," "disgust"
   definition: "fear," "horror"
3. context clues: "slowly," "stalked"
   definition: "seriously," "gravely"

Shall I Compare Thee to a Summer's Day? Page 78

Page 80

Finding the Main Idea

Sample response: The poem will make the beloved famous and remembered forever.

Page 81

Graphic Organizer: Sonnet

1. **Quatrain 1:** The speaker compares his beloved to a summer's day. Then, the speaker says that a summer's day can be stormy, and that summer passes.
2. **Quatrain 2:** Answer provided
3. **Quatrain 3:** The beloved's beauty will never fade. Death will not affect the speaker's beloved.
4. **Couplet:** The beloved will live as long as there are people who read this poem.

Night Calls Page 82

Page 84

Mood

Sample response: "stagnant," "covered with scum," "lonely letter," "frightened"

Page 85

Vocabulary

Sample response: The fact that the narrator does not go to school because she lives too far away helps me figure out that *remote* means "distant."

Monitoring Your Reading

The red-crested heron's arrival at the preserve convinces the narrator's father to stay.

Page 86

Vocabulary

"Running around outside" indicates that *frolicking* means "playing."

Monitoring Your Reading

The narrator's father has set the heron free.

Monitoring Your Reading

Sample response: For ten nights, the father follows the heron to check on its progress. When he doesn't hear it call one night, he becomes restless and sad.

Monitoring Your Reading

Sample response: The narrator mimics the heron's call so her father will think the heron is still alive. She does this because she knows her father is very attached to the heron and she doesn't want him to be upset by its death.

Page 88

Graphic Organizer: Mood

Sample responses follow.

1. Loneliness. Because the narrator's father doesn't hug her, it doesn't seem like they have a very close relationship.
2. Sadness. The images suggest that things in nature and in the narrator's father's life are at a standstill.
3. Loneliness. The narrator and her father do not seem to communicate about the mother's death or anything else.
4. Sadness/Hope. The sad call of the heron evokes a similar mood, but the father's hand movements seem to indicate a sense of hope.

Page 89

Vocabulary Development: Verifying Meanings by Examples

Sample responses follow.

1. If someone mimicked my speech, he or she copied it. Someone could also mimic a dog barking or a bird singing.
2. Dangers in a remote wilderness might include bad weather, wild animals, and a lack of food.
3. If someone is frolicking through a park, he or she might be skipping, running, or jumping.
4. If someone was waiting for something exciting to happen, he or she might feel restless. Someone might also feel restless if he or she had insomnia.

Call of the Wild—Save Us! Page 90

Page 92

Evaluating the Author's Argument

Sample response: A powerful word is being combined with an emotional appeal. No one wants to be a loser, and the headline says that we are all losers.

Page 93

Evaluating the Author's Argument

The author's claim is that something must be done now to prevent more species from becoming extinct. The article is a call to action.

Vocabulary

The underlined words should be "orders for money." Sample response: The sentence is asking us to support groups that help save wildlife. "Orders for money" is the only definition that fits the sentence.

Page 94

Graphic Organizer: Evaluating an Author's Argument

Sample responses follow.

Author's Intent: call to action
Facts/Statistics: "Half of the medicines we need come from wildlife species." "If the bill were about $2.5 billion a year, we would each pay just over $2 per year."
Loaded Words: Answer provided.
Logical Appeals: "It makes sense financially to save wildlife species."
Emotional Appeals: "We Are All Losers"
Tone: Concerned, forceful, persuasive.

Page 95

Vocabulary Development: Using Context Clues

1. Answer provided
2. species
3. vast
4. extinction
5. moral

My Sentence: Accept only an original sentence that includes underlined context clues that make the meaning of the word obvious.

Where Have You Gone, Charming Billy? Page 96

Page 99

Understanding Historical Context

Circled sentence: "He imagined Billy's father opening the telegram: SORRY TO INFORM YOU THAT YOUR SON BILLY BOY WAS YESTERDAY SCARED TO DEATH IN ACTION IN THE REPUBLIC OF VIETNAM."

Page 100

Vocabulary

Sample response: The word *stuck* means "stabbed."

Making Inferences

Sample response: Paul Berlin begins to laugh and can't stop. He makes up a story about life after the war. He is hysterical.

Page 101

Making Inferences

Sample response: I think Paul Berlin has learned that death can come at any instant, and in the most ridiculous fashion. He can't take anything for granted anymore.

Page 102

Graphic Organizer: Making Inferences

1. Inference: Paul Berlin cannot cope with what he saw.
   Explanation: Paul Berlin is pretending he didn't see Watkins die, which indicates that he is having trouble dealing with the death.

2. Inference: After a while, soldiers become numb to the violence of war.
   Explanation: The soldier is indicating that people get used to the violence eventually.
3. Inference: Berlin is hysterical.
   Explanation: Because Berlin cannot stop giggling or thinking about Watkins's death, it seems like he is not coping with his situation very well.
4. Inference: Berlin will always be haunted by the knowledge that he could die at any moment.
   Explanation: Judging by what Berlin has been through in the story, it seems as though the war has a profound effect on him.

Page 103

Vocabulary Development: Question and Answer

Sample responses are provided.
1. No. *Inert* means "not able to move."
2. No. *Paddy* means "field."
3. No. *Mines* are explosive devices.
4. Yes. *Medics* are people trained to give first aid on a battlefield.
5. No. In this context, *stuck* means Billy Boy was "stabbed" with a syringe.

The War Escalates /from Declaration of Independence from the War in Vietnam
Page 104

Page 107

Vocabulary

Circled words: "postponements of service."
Sample response: Rich men did not have to go to fight in Vietnam, mostly because they were going to college.

Balancing Viewpoints

Underlined words may include: "He was also poorer and had less education," "mostly because they were going to college," "served in combat in very high numbers," "faced terrible hardships," "faced the enemy in battles," "cut their way through jungles," "heard but did not see the enemy," and "faced the horrors of war daily."

Page 108

Balancing Viewpoints

"Almost 24 percent of all the battle deaths were African American."

Balancing Viewpoints

Circled words may be "madness," "poor," "suffering," "world which stands horrified at the path we have taken," and "stop the war."

Page 109

Graphic Organizer: Balancing Viewpoints

Sample responses are below.
1. King uses objective information to inform people of how the Vietnam War is affecting many poor American and Vietnamese people.

Fourth Course

2. King uses subjective information to persuade his readers to agree with his point of view.
3. Yes, King has a bias. King opposes the war because it takes men, skills, and money away from the struggle against poverty in the United States.

from The Tragedy of Julius Caesar Act I, Scene 2 Page 110

Page 112
Tragedy
Sample response: Antony seems to be very loyal to Caesar.

Page 113
Retelling
Sample response: Caesar dismisses the soothsayer as a dreamer and sends him away.

Vocabulary
"to ask for"

Page 114
Retelling
Sample response: Brutus says his troubled face is due to personal matters and that his friends should not be upset with him.

Page 115
Retelling
Sample response: Cassius is sorry that Brutus cannot see his own worth.

Page 116
Tragedy
Sample response: He fears that the people have made Caesar king. Even though he loves Caesar, he is against this.

Vocabulary
Sample response: When people ask me for a *favor*, it means they want me to do something for them.

Page 117
Vocabulary
Circled words should include two of the following: "troubled," "chafing," "her," or "angry."

Vocabulary
Sample response: The meaning of *bear* in line 14 is "to carry." Just as Aeneas carried his father on his back, Cassius carried Caesar on his own back.

Page 118
Retelling
Sample response: Caesar had a fever and a seizure in Spain. Cassius watched how Caesar shook and turned pale. Caesar's eyes became glazed, and Cassius heard Caesar groan.

Retelling
Sample response: Cassius says they have only themselves to blame for their troubles.

Page 119
Vocabulary
Sample response: The word *meet* can also mean "to encounter."

Page 120
Tragedy
Sample response: Brutus and Cassius do not want Caesar to become king. They plan to conspire against him.

Vocabulary
Train means "line of people." "All the rest" helped me figure this out.

Page 121
Retelling
Sample response: Caesar says he does not fear Cassius, but if a person like him *could* fear, he would definitely avoid Cassius.

Tragedy
Sample response: Caesar reveals that he thinks he is superior to most, if not all, men.

Page 122
Vocabulary
Sample response: I was *sad* when I got sick and had to miss the school field trip.

Page 123
Tragedy
Sample response: Casca doesn't respect the masses; he makes fun of their sweaty hats and stinking breath. Casca also reveals his distrust of Caesar's motives.

Page 124
Retelling
Sample response: Casca says that Caesar fainted. When Caesar woke up again, he said that if he had done or said anything strange, people should excuse him and blame it on his sickness. Three or four common women cried out that they forgave him with all their souls. But Casca said to ignore them, that if Caesar had stabbed their mothers, they would have said the same thing.

Page 125
Retelling
Sample response: They say that Casca has a lively personality and that he gets things done, despite his laid-back appearance.

Page 126
Retelling
Cassius says he can see that Brutus may be persuaded to join the conspiracy even though it goes against his nature.

Page 128

Graphic Organizer: Tragedy

Sample responses are below.

Main Characters: Julius Caesar, Brutus, Cassius
Conflicts: Is Caesar the defender or manipulator of the people? Cassius and Brutus plan to conspire against Caesar.
Setting: a public place in Rome
Background Information: Many people love Caesar, but some fear the possibility of his becoming king.

Page 129

Vocabulary Development: How to Own a Word

Accept any original sentences correctly using the vocabulary words.

Act III, Scene 2 Page 130

Page 133

Understanding Persuasion

Circled words may include "Roman(s)," "honor," "believe," "Caesar," "friend," "loved," "speak," and "offended."

Tragedy

Brutus is high ranking and he has a tragic lapse in judgment.

Page 134

Vocabulary

Sample response: I think the word *clamors* means "noises." A dictionary says that *clamors* can also mean "loud cries." Circled word: "shouts."

Page 135

Understanding Persuasion

Circled words: "Friends," "Romans," and "countrymen."

Vocabulary

Sample response: He wants the audience to listen to him.

Page 136

Understanding Persuasion

Sample response: Antony wants the crowd to believe that Brutus is *not* honorable.

Understanding Persuasion

Underlined words: "there is much reason in his sayings" and "Caesar has had great wrong."

Page 137

Vocabulary

Sample response: The meaning is "took note of; noticed." The plebeian is asking the others whether they took note of what Antony said.

Understanding Persuasion

Sample response: Antony wants the audience to riot against Brutus and Cassius.

Page 138

Understanding Persuasion

Antony is using props, or objects.

Vocabulary

Underlined meaning: "fitting and proper." Sample response: Let's meet at 5 P.M. to go to the movie.

Page 139

Understanding Persuasion

Underlined lines: "I fear I wrong the honorable men / Whose daggers have stabbed Caesar; I do fear it."

Understanding Persuasion

Circled words should include "traitors," "villains," and "murderers."

Page 140

Vocabulary

Sample response: I think *rent* means "a tear in cloth." This would make sense because Antony is displaying Caesar's torn and bloody cloak.

Page 141

Tragedy

This might be the turning point because the mob is frenzied and it seems like the conspirators' luck is about to turn.

Page 142

Understanding Persuasion

He would convince all of Rome to rebel.

Understanding Persuasion

Caesar's will

Page 143

Vocabulary

Sample response: The meaning of *brands* here is "pieces of burning wood" because the plebeian wants to use them to set fire to the traitors' houses.

Page 144

Understanding Persuasion

Possible response: His methods were unfair. He did not address Brutus's reasoning that Caesar was too ambitious. He stirred up the crowd by implying "honorable men" would never murder someone as great as Caesar.

Page 145

Graphic Organizer: Persuasion

Sample responses are below.
1. Emotional appeal: The sight of blood makes the Roman people angry at Caesar's murderers.
2. Props or Objects: Antony shows Caesar's will to the people.
3. Repetition: Antony's use of repetition shows that he really doesn't think Brutus is honorable.
4. Powerful Words: Antony's words get the people's attention.
5. Answer provided.

Fourth Course

Julius Caesar in an Absorbing Production Page 146

Page 148

Analyzing a Review
Underlined words may include: "Shakespeare no longer best suited for study in college" and "made Shakespeare's play interesting for ordinary people."

Vocabulary
Sample response: Groundlings are people who bought cheap tickets and stood on the ground in front of the stage. Many outdoor concerts today provide room for people to sit or stand in front of the stage.

Page 149

Analyzing a Review
Facts or judgments that back up the author's claim include Welles's creative direction, the use of sound, the characters, and the relevance of the play to the news of the day.

Page 150

Graphic Organizer: Analyzing a Review
1. Answer provided.
2. Sample response: Yes, I think Brown is qualified to write this review. He seems to know a lot about plays, actors, lighting, sound effects, and things like that. He is a reviewer for an important newspaper, so he is probably an expert.
3. Accept any aspect of the play used to support the writer's position, such as the direction, sound effects, and choice of actors.
4. Accept any reasonable answer and use it to encourage further research. Some students may want to read the play or a version of the play in order to find out how it was relevant to that historical period. Other students may be interested in viewing photographs of the production.
5. Accept any reasonable response.

Page 151

Vocabulary Development: Words in Context
1. **bury:** 2. to hide or cover up
2. **tragedy:** 1. a serious play that ends unhappily
3. **tragedy:** 2. a terrible happening
4. **thunder:** Answer provided.

Fifth Course

Answers to Annotations and Graphic Organizers

Encounters and Foundations to 1800
Page 2

Page 2
Vocabulary
Expeditions means "journeys for a purpose such as exploration."

Page 3
Vocabulary
Circle the context clues "jailed," "whipped," and "tortured." *Persecuted* means "cruelly oppressed, harmed, distressed, or hurt."

Page 4
Vocabulary
Circle "covenant" (line 65), "contract" (lines 65 and 69), and "Constitution" (line 70).

Page 5
Vocabulary
Tinkerers means "people who mend or patch up things."

Page 6
Vocabulary
Fuel is used here to mean "gave energy to."

Here Follow Some Verses upon the Burning of Our House, July 10, 1666
Page 8

Page 10
Inversion
The inverted words are "the light did spy." The arrow goes from "the light" to after "did spy." The normal English word order is: "I, starting up, did spy the light."

Page 11
Plain Style
Except for the inversions in lines 27 and 28, the style seems plain. The language is direct, and the words—such as *ashes, roof, guest,* and *table*—refer to simple, ordinary things.

Page 12
Vocabulary
Anne Bradstreet may use the word *pelf* to show her contempt for worldly belongings as compared with her love for God.

Page 14
Graphic Organizer: Poetic Inversion
1. when I took rest
2. I was wakened
3. Answer provided.
4. And I shall behold them no more.

Page 15
Vocabulary Development: Context Clues
1. Answer provided.
2. Circle *consumed*; underline "fire spread to the roof" and "whole building."
3. Circle *spy*; underline "hide-and-seek" and "saw anyone hiding."
4. Circle *store*; underline "boxes and bags of food" and "provisions that would see us through the winter."
5. Circle *framed*; underline "building" and "builder."

From Sinners in the Hands of an Angry God Page 16

Page 18
Figure of Speech
Underline "furnace of wrath" and "fire of God's anger."

Finding the Main Idea
Possible answer: The main idea of the sermon is that people cannot save themselves from God's anger; they are saved only by God's pleasure.

Page 19
Graphic Organizer: Figures of Speech
Possible meanings:
1. Answer provided.
2. God's anger is liked dammed waters because it is powerful and waiting to be released. God saves you by holding back his anger, but if he didn't, you would be destroyed.
3. God's anger is like a bow because it is tight and like an arrow because it is aimed at you and ready to fly. Justice bends the bow because it is only right that you should be destroyed because of your sins.
4. God, who is very angry, could easily send you to hell, just as you might drop an awful insect into a fire.

From The Autobiography (Franklin)
Page 20

Page 22
First-Person Point of View
Circle "Feeling much better" and "I was so tired."

Making Inferences
Possible answer: I can infer that Benjamin Franklin is very ambitious. He is also proud or naïve if he thinks he can become perfect.

Page 23
Making Inferences
Possible answer: The virtues are not listed in order of importance because they are all equally important. Students' choices of virtues to be added to or taken from the list will vary.

Vocabulary
Students' responses will vary.

Page 24
Making Inferences
Possible answer: The lines reveal Franklin's ambition, seriousness, and desire to improve himself.

Page 25
Graphic Organizer: First-Person Point of View
1. Franklin wanted to live without committing any fault at any time, but the task was more difficult than he had imagined.
2. Sometimes, while resisting one fault, Franklin was surprised to find himself committing another.
3. Answer provided.
4. Like a man with a large garden to weed, Franklin knew he could not get rid of all his faults at once.

Speech to the Virginia Convention
Page 26

Page 28
Recognizing Persuasion
Possible answers: Patrick Henry is appealing to logic when he says he judges "the future by the past" and when he describes the king's preparations for war. He is appealing to emotions when he uses words like *sly smile, trap, betrayed, kiss, darken, love, peace, fooled, war.*

Page 29
Recognizing Persuasion
Possible answer: Henry overwhelms listeners with questions they cannot answer, winning them over to his point of view.

Page 30
Recognizing Persuasion
The last lines are powerful because of their strong emotional appeal. Henry is willing to give his own life for liberty.

Page 31
Graphic Organizer: Persuasion
1. Henry is asking for facts that will justify the other men's hopes.
2. The word *chains* appeals to our fears of being chained or imprisoned.
3. Henry again asks for facts, specifically a date.
4. Answer provided.
5. Henry offers a powerful choice here: liberty or death.

The Autobiography: The Declaration of Independence Page 32

Page 34
Main Idea
Circle "all men are created equal."

Page 35
Parallelism
Circle "He has refused" four times.

Main Idea
Possible summary of main idea: The king has done many things to oppress the colonists.

Page 36
Parallelism
Underline "stolen from our ships," "burnt our towns," and "destroyed the lives of our people."

Main Idea
Responses should include two of the following actions: The colonists reminded the British of the history of their colonization, appealed to their sense of justice and nobility and to their family ties, and asked for their help.

Page 37
Graphic Organizer: Parallelism
Answers should include at least one of the following phrases for each item:
1. Answer provided.
2. "We have reminded"; "We have appealed"; "We have asked."
3. "to form alliances"; "to establish trade"; "to do all other acts."
4. "our fortunes"; "our sacred honor."

American Romanticism 1800–1860
Page 38

Page 39
Vocabulary
Escapism means "thinking about imaginary things to get away from everyday matters."

Page 40
Vocabulary
Backwoodsmen is made up of the three words *back, woods,* and *men.* It means "men who live or work deep in the woods."

Page 43
Vocabulary
Pasteboard means a "hard material made of layers of paper pasted together." A context clue is "masks," which are made of pasteboard.

Thanatopsis Page 44

Page 47
Reading Inverted Sentences
Yet a few days, and you shall see the all-beholding sun no more.

Theme

Underline at least "Earth . . . shall claim/Thy growth, to be . . . earth again . . . To mix forever with the elements,/To be a brother to the . . . rock/And to the . . . clod."

Page 48

Vocabulary

Vales means "valleys." The context clue is that the vales stretch between the hills.

Theme

Some students may find it comforting to be in such great company. Others may find no comfort in the thought, preferring a happier vision of an afterlife.

Page 49

Theme

Possible response: Live your life well, so you will die happily and without fear.

Page 51

Graphic Organizer: Theme Chart

Lines 1–17. Answer provided.

Lines 17–30. When you die, you become one with nature.

Lines 31–57. When you die, you join everyone who ever lived in a great tomb, which is all of nature.

Lines 58–72. Answer provided.

Lines 73–81. Live your life so you will welcome death unafraid.

Overall theme: Death is not frightening because it is a natural part of all life.

From Self-Reliance Page 52

Page 54

Understanding Metaphors

Possible answer: When plucked, iron strings vibrate powerfully. Emerson compares that vibration to how people feel about the idea "Trust yourself." It is very powerful.

Understanding Metaphors

Circle "blindly." Emerson is comparing people who accept society's beliefs and customs without thinking about them and deciding for themselves whether or not they are right to people who cannot see.

Page 56

Graphic Organizer: Metaphor

1. Imitation destroys a person's individuality.
2. People have a powerful positive response to the idea of trusting themselves.
3. Answer provided.
4. Unthinking people are scared into always behaving the same way.

Page 57

Vocabulary Development: Developing Vocabulary

Students' sentences will vary. Sample sentences:

1. I show self-reliance when I do my chores without being reminded.
2. Juliana shows her individuality in the way she dresses.
3. Getting along with others in school requires some conformity of behavior.
4. Class rules are constraints on individual behavior.
5. Answer provided.

From Resistance to Civil Government
Page 58

Page 60

Paradox

Thoreau sees a contradiction in his neighbors' stated opposition to slavery and the war in Mexico while they support these causes with their tax dollars.

Page 61

Asking Questions

Sample questions: How can just one person change a big country like the United States? How will it change society if I don't pay my taxes and get in trouble with the IRS?

Page 62

Paradox

Possible answers: Yes, when you are away in nature, you are free from governmental authority. No, the government is in control everywhere, with laws about behavior, land use, and so on.

Asking Questions

Sample questions: How do you think our government needs to change to become the government you imagine? Is such an ideal government really possible?

Page 63

Graphic Organizer: Paradox

1. Thoreau felt more free than his townsman because he was standing up for his beliefs.
2. The purpose of a government is to govern.
3. Thoreau paid his debt to society by going to jail.

The Minister's Black Veil Page 64

Page 66

Making Inferences

Students could answer "yes" or "no." If yes, underline "good preacher" (line 24). If no, underline "his method was mildly persuasive" (lines 24–25) and "He spoke softly" (line 25).

Page 67

Vocabulary

Presided means "was in the position of authority at an event."

Symbol
Possible response: I think Mr. Hooper is referring to death—when God sees and judges all your secret sins.

Page 68
Vocabulary
Toast means here a "drink in honor of someone or something."

Page 69
Symbol
Circle "gave up his usual walk" and "avoided mirrors."

Making Inferences
The veil convinced people that Mr. Hooper understood sin and death and could help them overcome sin and face death.

Page 70
Making Inferences
Possible response: The heart can be a prison if a person is alone or feels guilt.

Symbol
Possible answer: Mr. Hooper means that everyone is hiding their sins and not being open and honest.

Page 71
Graphic Organizer: Symbol
1. c
2. e
3. b
4. a
5. Answer provided.

The Pit and the Pendulum   Page 72

Page 74
Symbolic Meaning
The dark place deep below the earth may symbolize a grave, death, Hell, or despair.

Page 75
Retelling
The narrator is strapped to a wooden rack with only his head and an arm free so he can eat spicy food without anything to drink. Overhead there is a huge pendulum with a sharp blade that is swinging faster and faster and getting closer and closer to slicing the narrator in half.

Symbolic Meaning
At first, the rats symbolize horror, decay, and death, but after they gnaw through the narrator's straps, they may symbolize freedom or escape.

Page 76
Retelling
After the pendulum went away, the figures on the walls start to glow. The walls get fiery hot. Fearing he will burn up, the narrator rushes to the pit in the center of the room. He shrieks when he sees that the pit is full of rats gnawing bones. He weeps.

Symbolic Meaning
The arrival of the French army may symbolize freedom or God's pardoning of the damned.

Page 77
Graphic Organizer: Symbolic Meaning
1. Hell, death, a grave, despair
2. Death, punishment
3. Prison, torture
4. Answer provided.
5. Death, hellfires, torture
Symbolic meaning of the story: Poe is describing the inhumanity of the Spanish Inquisition and of any government that uses torture.

The Raven   Page 78

Page 81
Sound Effects
Circle "whispered" and "murmured."

Page 82
Sound Effects
Circle "ebony," "bird," "beguiling" and "sad," "fancy," "smiling."

Page 83
Sound Effects
Circle "muttered."

Interpreting a Poem
The speaker means that the Raven will leave in the morning, just as his other friends and all his hopes have already left him.

Page 84
Sound Effects
Draw arrows connecting "fowl" with "fiery" and "burned" with "bosom's."

Vocabulary
Methought sound like the words *me* and *thought*. *Methought* means "I thought."

Page 85
Interpreting a Poem
The speaker gets angry because the Raven said he will not be reunited in heaven with his beloved Lenore.

Vocabulary
Quoth reminds me of the word quote. *Quoth* means "quoted, or said."

Page 86
Interpreting a Poem
The raven never leaves and the speaker's spirits will never be lifted. This may symbolize the speaker's despair at the death of the woman he loves.

Page 87

Sound Effects

A. 1. Circle "silken," "sad," "uncertain," and "rustling."
   2. Answer provided.
   3. Circle "Doubting," "dreaming," "dreams," "dared," and "dream."
   4. Circle "Bird," "beast," "bust," "above," and "chamber."
   5. Circle "Tempter," "sent," "tempest," and "tossed."

B. Sample sentences:
   1. The bees buzzed among the rosebushes.
   2. Ahmed made a big splash when he dove into the pool.
   3. My dog always growls at the mail carrier.

American Masters: Whitman and Dickinson Page 88

Page 88

Vocabulary

Seams means here "the place where two pieces join." Underline "fabric," "uneven," and "tight."

From Song of Myself, Numbers 10, 33, and 52 Page 90

Page 93

Making Inferences

Underline "limpsy and weak," "sweated body and bruis'd feet," "galls of his neck and ankles," and "recuperated."

Free Verse

The sound repeated most often is *p*. Circle "perfectly," "putting," "plasters," "recuperated," and "pass'd."

Page 94

Making Inferences

The speaker means that he feels great empathy or sympathy for the captain and for the passengers on the wrecked ship; he feels a part of all humanity.

Page 95

Free Verse

Underline "condemn'd for a witch, burnt with dry wood, her children gazing on."

Free Verse

Circle "these" and "feel."

Free Verse

Underline "I am," "I wince," "I clutch," and "I fall."

Page 96

Making Inferences

By repeating "I am," Whitman is emphasizing the idea that he identifies with all people, or that we are all one.

Page 97

Free Verse

Circle "gurgles" and "gasps."

Making Inferences

He means the he will become part of nature, so he will be there when we walk on the earth or the grass.

Page 98

Free Verse

The sounds are *f*, *p*, *m*, and *s*. Circle, for *f*, "filter," "fiber," "failing," "fetch," and "first"; for *p*, "keep," "place," and "stop"; for *m*, "Missing," "me," and "somewhere"; and for *s*, "Missing," "search," "stop," and "somewhere."

Page 99

Graphic Organizer: Free Verse

1. b
2. Answer provided.
3. a
4. e
5. c

The Soul selects her own Society; Because I could not stop for Death
Page 100

Page 102

Vocabulary

Underline "superiority."

Slant Rhyme

They are slant rhymes.

Page 103

Irony

Underline "kindly" (line 2) and "Civility" (line 8). These words are ironic because we do not usually think of death as kindly or as civil.

Summarizing

Possible answers: The speaker and death passed the school where children were playing a game during recess; they passed fields full of ripe grain; they passed a sunset. Or, the speaker is remembering her whole life—her childhood, middle age, and old age.

Page 105

Graphic Organizer: Summary Chart

Possible summaries:
1. The speaker was too busy living to think of death, but death came to take her to eternal life.
2. Death was not in a hurry, and the speaker had stopped her work and recreation because she was dying.
3. Answer provided.
4. Dressed in only light clothes, the speaker grows cold.
5. They came to the speaker's gravesite.
6. The speaker has been dead for centuries that feel shorter than the day she died.

The Rise of Realism: The Civil War to 1914 Page 106

Page 107

Vocabulary
Underline "left on the battlefield for two or three days," "Conditions were not very clean," "medicine was primitive," and "A major wound led to amputation and even death."

Vocabulary
Circle "Aside from" and "rare." *Scant* means "small; barely enough."

Page 108

Vocabulary
Underline "perform."

Vocabulary
Underline "wanted to give readers a close, hard look at real life" and "It also tried to explain *why* people behave the way they do."

Page 109

Vocabulary
Straight-laced once meant "wearing tightly laced clothes," but it now means "narrowly strict in morals or behavior." The world suggests that Howe's fiction is narrow and judgmental about human behavior.

Page 110

Vocabulary
Underline "His books are concerned with exploring people's motivation—why they do what they do" or "he believed that human motives are rooted in the human mind."

Narrative of the Life of Frederick Douglass Page 112

Page 114

Analyzing a Writer's Purpose
Underline "On one of the hottest days of the month of August 1833," "About three o'clock," "When I could not long stand up," and "immediately."

Page 115

Analyzing a Writer's Purpose
Possible response: Douglass's purpose was to elicit the reader's sympathy.

Page 116

Analyzing a Writer's Purpose
Possible response: It was unusual and dangerous for enslaved people to fight their owners, so Douglass may have been surprised when he looked back at his own courage and may not have known where it came from.

Metaphor
Circle "bloody arm of slavery." It means that slavery is brutal to enslaved people.

Page 117

Graphic Organizer: Metaphor
1. A heart is compared to something made of iron. It means that even a hard, uncaring person would have felt sympathy for him because of the way he looked.
2. Answer provided.
3. Slavery is compared to a person with a bloody arm. It means that slavery is very oppressive.

A Mystery of Heroism Page 118

Page 120

Situational Irony
It is ironic to chop up a house for firewood because we expect houses to be places of safety and warmth; chopping them down destroys the safety in order to produce another kind of warmth.

Page 121

Summarizing
When Collins is teased for wanting water, he asks his captain if he can get some from a well that is in the middle of a battle. The captain tries to discourage him, but agrees to his going.

Situational Irony
Collins's decision is surprising because people usually try to protect themselves, but Collins is risking death just for a drink of water.

Page 122

Situational Irony
Possible responses: The overall irony is that people often expect war to be heroic, but it full of horrors. Or, in war people may do very brave things for very foolish reasons.

Page 123

Graphic Organizer: Situational Irony
1. Answer provided.
2. Collins decides to get the water when his comrades tease and dare him.
3. Collins doesn't know why he is getting the water.
4. The lieutenants joke around and spill the water, making Collins's sacrifice pointless.

The Gettysburg Address Page 124

Page 126

Analyzing a Writer's Style
Circle "nation" (lines 2, 5, and 8) and "dedicate/d" (lines 2, 5, and 7). Underline "so conceived" and "so dedicated" and also "we are engaged," "We are met," and "We have come."

Page 127

Analyzing a Writer's Style
Underline "of the people, by the people, for the people." These phrases remind the audience what democracy really is and how important it is to all people.

Fifth Course

Page 128

Graphic Organizer: Style
1. Answer provided.
2. The parallel structure gives a powerful rhythm to the speech. The phrases have similar meanings, but move from the more everyday to the more sacred.
3. The repetition stresses the importance of the dedication they are making on that day.

Page 129

Vocabulary Development: Developing Vocabulary
Sample answers:
1. Answer provided.
2. Nicole conceived a plan for the class picnic.
3. They planned to consecrate the new house of worship.
4. People wanted to hallow the ground where the soldiers had died.

To Build a Fire Page 130

Page 132

Analyzing Cause and Effect
A person without imagination may not be able to realize the possible dangers of a situation and might therefore take risks that lead to trouble.

Naturalism
Underline "its instinct told the dog how cold it really was" and "The cold depressed the dog. It wanted the man to stop and make camp or build a fire."

Page 133

Naturalism
Underline "The man took off a mitten" or "In less than a minute the man's exposed fingers grew numb."

Page 134

Vocabulary
Old-timer means a "person who has been around a long time."

Page 135

Analyzing Cause and Effect
Underline "he could smell the flesh of his hands burning."

Naturalism
The dog recognizes danger in the man's voice and does not come when the man calls him.

Page 136

Analyzing Cause and Effect
He decides to die with dignity and thinks that sleep is a good way to die.

Naturalism
Possible responses: Nature doesn't care about human beings; people should respect nature and be careful; humans cannot survive alone in a harsh environment.

Page 137

Graphic Organizer: Cause and Effect
Possible causes and effects:
Cause: The man takes off his gloves to help the dog.
Effect: His fingers become numb.

Cause: The man falls into icy water.
Effect: He builds a fire to dry off.

Cause: The man builds the fire under a tree.
Effect: The snow on the branches melts and puts out the fire.

Cause: The man tries to build a new fire with numb hands.
Effect: He is too clumsy to get the fire going.

Cause: The man plans to kill the dog and calls it over.
Effect: The dog hears danger in the man's voice and stays away.

Cause: The man realizes he is going to die.
Effect: He decides to sleep and die with dignity.

Cause: The man freezes to death.
Effect: The dog leaves to find food and a fire elsewhere.

A Pair of Silk Stockings Page 138

Page 140

Analyzing Historical Context
Underline "silk stockings," "two dollars and fifty cents to one dollar and ninety-eight cents." Mrs. Sommers's life is similar to women's today in that women today may also know the value of bargains and fights crowds to get them. It is different in that shoppers got more service in her day than they usually do today, women wore silk stockings instead of nylons, and the costs of goods were generally lower.

Page 141

Motivation
Possible response: Mrs. Sommers feels free from responsibility because she has just made an extravagant purchase for herself and is enjoying it.

Analyzing Historical Context
Underline "skirts," "pointed-tipped boots," "gloves," "long kid glove." Like Mrs. Sommers, women still wear skirts and boots, but today they usually wear gloves only for warmth, not for appearance. Mrs. Sommers's skirt is long, but women today wear pants or skirts of many different lengths.

Page 142

Motivation
Mrs. Sommers usually eats at home to save money. She decides to eat in a restaurant today because she is treating herself to nice things instead of saving the money for her family.

Page 143

Motivation

Mrs. Sommers wants the cable car ride to go on forever because she has enjoyed her day of extravagance and doesn't want it to end.

Page 144

Graphic Organizer: Motivation

1. Mrs. Sommers loves her children and wants the best for them.
2. Answer provided.
3. In her youth, Mrs. Sommers was used to fine things. She wants the best now that she has decided to treat herself.
4. Mrs. Sommers was worried people would think she was not dressed well enough for such a nice restaurant.
5. Going to the theater is such a rare treat for Mrs. Sommers that she is really enjoying it.

Page 145

Vocabulary Development: Synonyms and Antonyms

gaunt: Answer provided.

gaudy—synonym: bright, showy; antonym: plain, simple.

leisurely—synonym: slow; antonym: fast.

luxurious—synonym: rich, splendid, comfortable; antonym: poor, cheap, ordinary.

The Moderns: 1914–1939 Page 146

Page 148

Vocabulary

Underline "show the moment-by-moment flow of their characters' thoughts."

Vocabulary

Prohibition means an "order or law that forbids something."

Page 149

Vocabulary

Circle "Symbolists believed that striking images were more powerful than direct statements of feeling."

Winter Dreams Page 150

Page 152

Motivation

Dexter dreams of living a high-class life. He wants to be a member of the golf club, not its caddy. Judy Jones represents the life he aspires to and he wants to impress her, so both are motivations for his quitting the caddy job.

Page 153

Making Inferences

Possible response: Judy is spoiled and uses people for her own pleasure. She is used to having them do what she wants, but she gets bored if they are too admiring.

Page 154

Making Inferences

Underline "I've been mad about loads of poor men and fully intended to marry them all" and "my interest in him wasn't strong enough."

Page 155

Motivation

Underline "he was playing with the idea of going East to New York and taking Judy Jones with him" and "No reality could make her anything but desirable to him."

Page 156

Making Inferences

Underline "After a week of misery and hard work," and "he thought the young and already fabulously successful Dexter Green should know more about such things." Dexter is hard-working and sticks to his work even when he is unhappy. He is impressed with his own success but recognizes what he doesn't know and wants to learn it. He is very ambitious and hopes to raise himself up socially.

Motivation

Possible responses: Judy thinks Dexter is hers and doesn't want someone else to get him. She wants to get him back just to prove that she can.

Page 157

Making Inferences

Dexter is escaping the complications in his life—his loss of Judy Jones as well as work and social pressures, perhaps.

Making Inferences

Perhaps when Judy Jones finally married she felt committed to her husband. She may have loved him enough to be willing to be hurt by him. She may also have cared more about her children than about conquering men.

Page 158

Making Inferences

The thing that "will come back no more" is Dexter's dream about the good life. When Judy no longer represents that dream, it loses its luster. The dream itself no longer delights Dexter.

Page 159

Graphic Organizer: Making Inferences

1. Answer provided.
2. Judy uses people. She gets bored with people who admire her too much.
3. Dexter has a lot of ambition, but he is unrealistic about Judy Jones.

4. Judy is spoiled, selfish, and thinks only of herself.
5. Once she marries and settles down, Judy loses her power to attract men.

A Rose for Emily Page 160

Page 163
Setting
Underline "As if any man could keep a kitchen properly" and "Will you accuse a lady of smelling bad?" Possible responses: Men and women had different roles. Gentlemen were courteous to and protective of women.

Making Inferences About Character
The townspeople resent it when the Griersons feel superior. They feel more sympathetic when they learn Miss Emily is no longer rich and is therefore more like them.

Page 164
Making Inferences About Character
Underline "Yankee," "rough good looks," "laughing," and "center of the group." Homer Barron is a rugged, cheerful, popular man.

Making Inferences About Character
Miss Emily is proud and knows how to get her way.

Setting
At the time, it was thought that a woman was no longer respectable if she went out with a man unchaperoned and he didn't marry her. If a woman lost her reputation, it was thought she might as well kill herself.

Page 165
Making Inferences About Character
Miss Emily was sleeping with the corpse years after the murder. Perhaps she didn't want anyone else to leave her. After the murder she was unable to accept Homer Barron's death and wanted to believe he was still with her.

Page 166
Graphic Organizer: Setting
1. Answer provided.
2. The townspeople followed traditional customs.
3. The townspeople were snobbish and looked down on people from the North and on laborers.
4. The townspeople were curious about their neighbors, but respected their privacy.

Page 167
Vocabulary Development: Multiple-Meaning Words
1. b
2. d
3. Answer provided.
4. b
5. d

Nobel Prize Acceptance Speech, 1950
Page 168

Page 170
Public Speaking
Circle "old truths" and "old universal truths."

Finding the Main Idea
Underline "by listing his heart" and "by reminding him of the courage and honor and hope and pride and compassion and pity and sacrifice that have been the glory of his past."

Page 171
Graphic Organizer: Public Speaking
1. Underline "not" and "but." Circle "Contrast."
2. Answer provided.
3. Underline "by lifting his heart" and "by reminding him." Circle "Parallelism."

A Worn Path Page 172

Page 174
Theme
Circle "noises," "wild animals," "thorn bush," "rushing creek," "barbed-wire fence," and "buzzard."

Page 175
Making Predictions
Circle "I'm going to town" (line 44), "I have to go to town" (line 46), "big building" (lines 62 and 64), "many steps" (line 64), and "a door" (line 65). Possible response: I think Phoenix is going to an office of some kind, perhaps to apply for assistance because she seems very poor.

Page 176
Making Predictions
Underline "she comes to get medicine for her grandson." Students will probably have predicted other reasons. Possible responses: The reason was not revealed earlier in order to keep the reader in suspense or to keep the focus on Phoenix and her journey of love.

Theme
Phoenix has given her grandson gifts of love, caring, and the medicine, which she walks very far to get. I think the theme is about how much people will do for love.

Page 17
Graphic Organizer: Theme
1. A phoenix burns itself and then rises from its own ashes. This relates to overcoming obstacles over and over again.
2. The whole story is about Phoenix's journey for love, which she makes over and over.
3. Answer provided.
4. As soon as she gets two nickels, Phoenix plans to spend them on the grandson she loves.

Contemporary Literature: 1939 to Present Page 178

Page 178
Vocabulary
The nuclear bomb's mushroom cloud represents the destructive side of science and technology, the fears of the cold war, and the threat of a nuclear war that could destroy the planet.

Page 179
Vocabulary
In line 47, *play* means "freedom of possibility."

Page 183
Vocabulary
Transcendentalists believed that to find the truth, you had to transcend, or go beyond, the everyday experiences of the physical world. They believed that humanity could be perfected.

The Way to Rainy Mountain Page 184

Page 186
Setting
Circle "Black Hills." The writer travels to the Black Hills to see the place where his ancestors came from, which his grandmother often described but had never seen.

Page 187
Setting
The indoor setting is inside his grandmother's house.

Page 188
Main Ideas and Supporting Details
Underline "Once there was a lot of sound in my grandmother's house, a lot of coming and going, feasting and talk." Circle "Visitors came in the summer," "There were prayer meetings," "great nighttime feasts," "We children played outside," "singing," "good things to eat," and "a lot of laughter."

Setting
Underline "silence in the rooms of her house," "sat a long time on the stone steps," "strange thing," "looking like a fossil," "to live and die," "its smallness was made large and eternal," "longing deep within me," "shadows," "grave," "ancestral names," and "Looking back." Possible responses: The mood is thoughtful, nostalgic, sad, longing, and reverent.

Page 189
Graphic Organizer: Setting
1. uplifting, spiritual, proud. Rainy mountain is a harsh land with extreme weather. It is a lonely land that brings thoughts of Creation.
2. Answer provided.
3. cheerful, vibrant, full of life. Many people visited. There was a lot of laughter, song, prayer, and feasting.
4. Quiet, sad, full of memories and longing. The house is silent. The writer sits and looks at the moon and remembers.

Sixth Course

Answers to Annotations and Graphic Organizers

The Anglo-Saxons 449–1066 Page 2

Page 2

Vocabulary

The Britons were a group within the Celts. Their name was used to name their land—Britain.

Page 3

Vocabulary

Words to be underlined are "Angles" and "Saxons." The language and people are both called Anglo-Saxon.

Page 5

Vocabulary

Bards are people who entertained the Anglo-Saxons with songs and stories about gods and heroes. Their job was to help people remember the deeds and adventures of heroes.

Words to be circled include "sing to the strumming of a harp," "tales of gods and heroes charmed and delighted audiences," "a way for . . . their heroic deeds to be remembered," and "job of the bard to preserve a person's fame in song."

Vocabulary

The word *havens* means "safe places."
The word *monasteries* should be underlined.

Page 6

Vocabulary

Scribes means "people who write." The words "writing," "copying," "texts," and "writing room" helped me figure out this meaning.

The Battle with Grendel Page 8

Page 10

Epic Hero

Words that may be underlined or listed include "forever joyless," "snapped it open," "Tore its iron fasteners with a touch," "rushed angrily," "snarling," "fierce," "eyes / Gleamed in the darkness," "burned with a gruesome / Light," "Intended to tear the life from those bodies," and "monster's mind was hot / With the thought of food and the feasting his belly / Would soon know."

Page 11

Epic Hero

Words to be underlined are "seized" and "Beowulf leaned up on one arm."

Vocabulary

The word *flooded* means "overwhelmed by a flow or movement of something."

In the text, *flooded* shows that Grendel felt a lot of fear move through him. There is no mention of water in line 44 or in the lines before or after it.

Page 13

Epic Hero

Grendel had put a spell on all the men's weapons, blunting every mortal man's blade.

Beowulf did not use a weapon; he tore Grendel apart with his bare hands.

Page 14

Vocabulary

Words to be underlined include "bleeding sinews . . . / Snapped," "muscle and bone split / And broke."

Epic Hero

Beowulf hung Grendel's arm from the rafters.

Page 15

Vocabulary

The word *murky* means "hard to see through" or "dark." The words that help with the meaning are "hidden," "deep," and "darkness."

Epic Hero

The phrase "warrior worthier to rule over men" best describes Beowulf.

Page 16

Graphic Organizer: Epic Hero

Sample responses are provided.

1. Answer provided.
2. "Bold and strong-minded, had driven affliction / Off, purged Herot clean"
3. "retelling / Beowulf's bravery as they jogged along"

Beowulf is described as being bold, strong-minded, concerned about others, and brave.

Accept any reasonable explanation of how the selected images lead to the student's understanding of Beowulf's heroic nature.

Page 17

Vocabulary Development:

Anglo-Saxon Words and Word Parts

Sample responses are provided.

a– apart
be– begrudge
for– forgive
mis– mistake
over– overburden
un– unlikely

from Gilgamesh: A Verse Narrative
Page 18

Page 21

Responding to the Text

Sample responses provided.

Humbaba is begging for his life. Humbaba is offering to be Gilgamesh's slave. Gilgamesh is pausing long enough to let Humbaba plead and beg.

Conflict

Humbaba does not want to die, and Gilgamesh wants to kill Humbaba. Gilgamesh wants to kill the monster, but this conflicts with the possibility that the monster Humbaba could become Gilgamesh's servant.

Page 22

Responding to the Text

Some students may respond that hanging Humbaba's head from a tree is a good ending for the story because the times were brutal and cruel. Other students may find the ending too brutal and cruel and suggest another ending.

Page 23

Graphic Organizer: Conflict

Gilgamesh: Lines 42–45, internal; Enkidu: Lines 19–20, internal; Humbaba: Lines 24–30, external.

The Middle Ages 1066–1485 Page 24

Page 25

Vocabulary

Chivalry is a particular way of behaving. It is based on loyalty, bravery, and courtly behavior. The word *courtly* in line 45 should be mentioned.

Vocabulary

Course means "the direction that something takes." The sentence says that "major events changed the course of English history and literature." When the word *direction* is substituted for *course*, the meaning of the sentence stays the same. Substituting "a series of studies" does not make sense.

Page 26

Vocabulary

The punctuation is the dash. The phrase "someone who dies for his or her beliefs" should be underlined in line 88.

Page 27

Vocabulary

The word *curb* means "hold back." The barons wanted to hold back the power of the king. There is no mention of concrete or an edge in these sentences.

from The Canterbury Tales Page 28

Page 31

Characterization

The Knight's fine horses and his coarse, worn, and stained clothing suggest a plain, modest man who is well off but who cares little about impressing others.

Vocabulary

The word *render* means "give."

Page 32

Analyzing Key Details

The Nun sings through her nose. Though she speaks French, her French is not "real" French as spoken in Paris.

Characterization

The Nun is extremely careful about her table manners, and she eats in a refined way. She puts on airs of courtly grace, but to anyone watching her, her manners might seem to be phony. She doesn't drop food down her front, she does not dip her fingers too deeply in the sauce, and she wipes her mouth so that she doesn't leave grease on the cup when she drinks. She doesn't grab at the meat but reaches out slowly and sedately.

Page 33

Analyzing Key Details

Some students will answer that the Nun has a pretty face. Details include an elegant nose and a soft, red mouth. Others will say that she is not pretty—she has glass-gray eyes, an extremely small mouth, and a wide forehead.

Page 34

Characterization

The details suggest that the monk loves material pleasures—he likes to hunt, does not think he should stay in his cloister, does not like to study, owns greyhounds, hunts hares, and wears rich clothes and jewelry.

Page 35

Analyzing Key Details

The Oxford Cleric's coat is threadbare; he doesn't have a job; he prefers to buy books rather than clothes, or a fiddle or other stringed instrument, such as a psaltery, to make music.

Page 37

Analyzing Key Details

The Doctor is greedy and dishonest; he prescribes unnecessary medicines and gets a kickback from the apothecaries.

Vocabulary

The word *guile* suggests that they are sneaky. Both the Doctor and the apothecaries are cheating the patients.

Page 38

Characterization

The Wife of Bath cares more about status than about spiritual values. Some students may also respond that she is overeager to marry.

Analyzing Key Details

The names of places indicate that the Wife of Bath has traveled to many places, so she is very active. This travel probably costs a lot of money, so she is well off. Traveling to shrines was probably the "in" thing to do.

Page 39
Characterization
Words to be underlined include "holy-minded man," "good renown," "rich in holy thought and work," "learned," "truly knew Christ's gospel," and "teach."

Page 40
Vocabulary
Words that mean about the same as *disdainful* include "contemptuous" and "too proud or fine." Words to be circled may include "holy and virtuous," "discreet in teaching," and "benign."

Vocabulary
Words to be underlined should include "He put to sharp rebuke."

Page 41
Characterization
The words "driblets," "rat-tails," and "no hood upon his head" should be underlined.

Page 42
Vocabulary
The words *harbor* and *harbored* show that a beard has never grown and never will grow on the chin of the Pardoner. When a ship is anchored in a port, it is harbored there.

The words "chin no beard" are the biggest clue to the speaker's meaning.

Characterization
The author directly tells the reader that the Pardoner reads a lesson, tells a story, and sings an Offertory well. He implies that the Pardoner is motivated by greed and sings for pay—to "win silver from the crowd."

Page 43
Graphic Organizer: Characterization
Responses comparing a pilgrim with three people students know will vary. Accept only those responses that are supported with details from the text.

Federigo's Falcon Page 44

Page 47
Vocabulary
The meaning of *support* in line 35 is "provide for." The falcon hunts for food for Federigo. There is no mention of anyone or anything falling down.

Evaluating the Historical Context
Yes, the language used by the couple shows that the story is happening in the past. Their speech is formal and extremely polite.

Situational Irony
In his attempt to please Monna Giovanna with something trivial—a nice meal—Federigo has prevented himself from doing her a much greater favor.

Page 48
Situational Irony
Ironically Federigo's generosity in killing his falcon finally leads to his marriage to Monna Giovanna. Having lost his fortune courting his lady, Federigo gets her and her fortune in the end.

Page 49
Graphic Organizer: Plot
Sample responses provided.

Exposition: Answer provided.
Conflict: Federigo's hopeless love for Monna Giovanna. Federigo's hopeless poverty.
Complications: Answer provided.
Climax: Federigo's killing and serving the falcon for a meal.
Resolution: Marriage of Monna Giovanna and Federigo.

The Renaissance Page 50

Page 51
Vocabulary
The word *press* in line 41 refers to "a machine that prints out newspapers, books, or magazines." None of the other definitions can be substituted for *press* in line 41. Also, the discussion in lines 37–42 is about printing books mechanically—by machine—rather than by hand.

Vocabulary
The word *flood* in line 42 means "a great supply" because "great supply" can be substituted for "flood" in the sentence and the sentence will still have the same meaning.

Page 52
Vocabulary
The word *subjects* means "people who are under one authority" and refers to the people who are ruled by King Henry. Some other meanings for *subjects* include "courses of study," "parts of sentences," "topics," "things or persons tested," and "musical or literary themes."

Page 53
Vocabulary
Synonyms for *feuds* include "quarrels," "fights," and "wars."

Page 54
Vocabulary
The word *plots* means "secret plans" in line 136. The life of Elizabeth I was in danger, so secret plans of murder would fit in this sentence. There is nothing about land or stories.

Page 55

Vocabulary

"Spoke poorly" should be underlined. The meaning of *eloquent* is "well spoken."

Vocabulary

Dictator means "ruler." The word *ruled* helps the student arrive at this meaning.

Meditation 17 Page 56

Page 59

Vocabulary

Underlined words should include "death," "misery," "pain," "misfortune," "trouble," and "suffering."

Page 60

Graphic Organizer: Tone

Sample responses provided.
1. Serious; details: death imagery, bells tolling, sickness.
2. Hopeful; details: images of connectedness, "no one person is an island."

Page 61

Vocabulary Development: Word Maps

Answers will vary.

Tilbury Speech page 62

Page 64

Understanding Persuasive Techniques

Elizabeth compares herself to a king.
She is saying that she is as strong as any king.

Page 65

Graphic Organizer: Persuasion

Sample responses provided.
1. Answer provided.
2. This comparison projects a favorable image of Elizabeth as a just ruler.
3. An emotional appeal emphasizes the queen's courage and devotion to the nation and to her subjects.
4. This use of comparison and contrast reminds the people that she is strong and courageous.
5. This use of cause and effect—you fight, I reward you—provides a practical, concrete incentive for the people to follow her into battle.

The Parable of the Prodigal Son
Page 66

Page 69

Graphic Organizer: Parable

Possible responses are given.
1. God
2. repentant sinners
3. envy

The Restoration and the 18th Century
Page 70

Page 71

Vocabulary

The word *calculate* means "figure out." Halley used math to figure out, not guess, at the length of a comet's orbit.

Page 72

Vocabulary

Underlined words and phrases connected to the word *sordid* should include "sloppiness," "bad behavior," "bad taste," "worst of human nature," and "underside."

Page 73

Vocabulary

Defoe thought that what he wrote could change society.

Vocabulary

Underlined words should include "unlucky people" and "rambling, comical adventures."

Page 74

Vocabulary

Inspiration means "being moved to create something." The paragraph in which this word appears is telling where writers get new ideas for their writing. There is nothing about breathing.

A Modest Proposal Page 76

Page 78

Vocabulary

The meaning of *burden* in line 2 is "something that you have to put up with."

Page 79

Recognizing Persuasive Techniques

The narrator uses a logical appeal, citing the statistics of how many people a twenty-eight-pound child might feed and the ways to cook a child to make it last several days.

The word *child* used here when discussing the cooking of meat is an emotional appeal.

Page 80

Vocabulary

The narrator is talking about humans as if they were animals. The word *slaughter* is generally used to refer to the killing of animals or to describe a terrible way to kill humans.

Verbal Irony

The narrator says that some people might think that killing males and females is cruel and that he would never be cruel. He is using irony by pretending to be kind. He is actually being cruel, because his plan for eating children is cruel.

Recognizing Persuasive Techniques

Underlined facts should include three of the following: "cut down on the number of Roman Catholics," "poor tenants will now have valuable property," "it will help the economy," "breeders will earn money," "popular new dish will draw wealthy customers to taverns," "it would encourage mothers to take good care of their children," and "men would value their pregnant wives."

Page 81

Vocabulary

Solutions means "the answers to problems." It can also mean "liquids in which something is dissolved."

Verbal Irony

The narrator's statement is ironic because his proposal—eating the children—is evil, while his motive—saving adults and children from suffering and death—is good.

Page 82

Graphic Organizer: Irony

Sample responses provided.
1. Answer provided.
2. The author actually means hopeless, the opposite of hopeful.
3. The narrator's proposal is savage and barbaric. He has no children of his own, so his proposal won't affect him.

Page 83

Vocabulary Development: Word Analogies
1. b
2. d

from Don Quixote   Page 84

Page 87

Making Inferences

Sancho Panza is much more level-headed and logical than Don Quixote.

Vocabulary

Club means "a heavy stick used as a weapon." Context clues include "heavy oak branch" and "pounded his enemies with it in battle."

Parody

Don Quixote doesn't complain about any of his injuries. He suffers in silence instead. He also goes without sleep all night so he can think about the woman he loves.

Page 89

Graphic Organizer: Parody

Sample answers are provided.
1. the ferocity of the windmills
2. Don Quixote says statements such as "Clearly, you don't know much about this kind of adventure" (line 11) to Sancho Panza when in reality, the servant is far more sensible than Don Quixote.

3. the pairing of Don Quixote and Sancho Panza
4. The fight with the windmills is a humorous imitation of a real battle.

The Romantic Period   Page 90

Page 90

Vocabulary

Underlined words should include "changing rapidly," "growing restless," and "rebelled."

Page 91

Vocabulary

The tyrant is Napoleon.

Vocabulary

Underlined words should be "French words mean 'let people do as they please'" and "buying and selling should be allowed to happen without government interference." Groups of people affected include the rich, the helpless, and the young.

Page 93

Vocabulary

The correct meaning of *role* is "purpose or proper work." The paragraph in which the word *role* appears describes the types of work done by poets.

Vocabulary

The meaning of *in sum* is "in summary." *Sum* is part of the word *summary*, and a sum is the answer when you add up numbers. The previous paragraph lists all the qualities of the Romantic poet. "Someone we cannot do without" is the sum of all these qualities.

Lines Composed a Few Miles Above Tintern Abbey   Page 94

Page 96

Recognizing Patterns of Organization

An indentation shows where one stanza—or verse paragraph—ends and another begins.

Page 98

Recognizing Patterns of Organization

The speaker is talking directly to the river. Line 56, "O sylvan Wye! thou wanderer . . ." is the line that gives you the best clue.

Page 100

Blank Verse

When reading it aloud or to yourself, pronounce the word *power* as if it had only one syllable (*pow'r*).

Recognizing Patterns of Organization

Sample response: The poet or speaker loves nature because it helps him to be a better person.

Page 102
Blank Verse
Line 116: "dear," "Friend," "in," "voice," "catch," and so on. If possible, have students demonstrate this technique.

Page 105
Graphic Organizer: Blank Verse
Sample responses provided.
- Verse paragraph 2 is unified by the description of the value of memories for the speaker.
- Verse paragraph 3 describes how often the speaker relies on these memories.
- Verse paragraph 4 gives the history of the speaker's responses to nature.
- Verse paragraph 5 returns to the presence of the speaker's sister and to the landscape as experienced through her.

Kubla Khan   Page 106

Page 109
Alliteration
Line 37, the **d** sound in **d**ulcimer and **d**amsel
Lines 37 and 40, the word "dulcimer" repeats the **d** sound
Line 43, **s**ymphony and **s**ong; line 44, **s**uch
Line 44, **d**eep and **d**elight

Responding to the Poem
Sample response: The image is of a person's face with bright, flashing eyes. The hair is flying out around the face and going around the person three times. The hair is long. The face is dreadful because of the power of the honeydew and the milk of Paradise, which the person has eaten and drunk.

Most students will pick up on the dangerous aspects of this image and feel afraid. Others may feel curiosity. Students may question the identity of the figure, why the speaker tells the reader to close his or her eyes "with holy dread," and the nature of the "milk of paradise."

Page 110
Graphic Organizer: Alliteration
1. "**d**id," "**d**ome," "**d**ecree"; "**r**iver," "**r**an"; "**m**easureless," "**m**an"; "**s**unle**ss**," "**s**ea"
2. The consonant sound **c** should be circled in "**c**lasps," "**c**rag," and "**c**roo**k**ed."
3. Accept only a response in which alliteration is used to clearly describe a person or place.

Page 111
Vocabulary Development: Developing Vocabulary
Sentences should contain context clues that reveal the meanings of the words.
Sample responses provided.
1. *Enfolding* the kittens in her arms every evening, she lavished love on the small creatures.

2. By the middle of the month, the *waning* moon had dwindled to a crescent.

The Victorian Period   Page 112

Page 112
Vocabulary
Sample responses: Homophones for *reign* are *rain* and *rein*.
The word *reign* means "period of power."

Page 113
Vocabulary
Phrases that should be underlined include "the vote to almost all adult males" and "limited the length of the workday for children."

Vocabulary
A result of making education compulsory was that by 1900, more than 90 percent of the English population could read and write.

Page 114
Vocabulary
Words that should be underlined are "Through his own effort and talent, he rose from poverty to wealth and fame," "happy endings," and "things usually work out well for decent people."

Vocabulary
Underlined words should include "smoke," "fire," "industrial landscapes," and "storm-cloud."

Page 115
Vocabulary
Underlined words should include "Lovers and friends are hurt and betrayed by human troubles," "unfaithfulness," "war," and "natural troubles (such as death)."

Vocabulary
Sample response: The smaller word *contradict,* which means "say or do the opposite," helps me figure out that *contradictions* are things that are the opposite of what people believe are true.

Ulysses   Page 116

Page 118
Vocabulary
Accept any reasonable sentence using the word *dole.*

Page 119
Vocabulary
Phrase to be underlined is "not to shine."
Sample response: The definition of *unburnished* is "not shiny," or "dull."

Page 120

Comparing and Contrasting

Telemachus appears to respect convention; he willingly does what is expected of him. He is characterized by "slow prudence" and "soft degrees." Ulysses, on the other hand, was once, and still desires to be, spontaneous, adventurous, resourceful, and unconventional.

Page 121

Comparing and Contrasting

Ulysses identifies with his companions and their exploits. He feels close to them. Ulysses may love and even admire his son, but he does not want to be like him.

Page 122

Theme

Sample response: Ulysses says that although he is growing older and is not as strong as he used to be, he wants to continue to live life to its fullest.

Page 123

Graphic Organizer: Theme

Sample responses are provided.
1. These lines bring out Ulysses' questing personality and his determination to live life to the fullest.
2. This passage reflects Ulysses' wish to put his talents and abilities to full use.
3. Answer provided.
4. This passage reflects Ulysses' conviction that even in old age, people can make use of their potential.

The Bet Page 124

Page 126

Theme

Sample response: The lawyer thinks any life is better than death, even one spent in prison. This indicates that the lawyer values life very highly.

Page 127

Making Predictions

Sample response: Religion may provide the lawyer with a sense of hope that will make him feel happier.

Page 128

Vocabulary

Fowl.

Page 129

Vocabulary

"Despise" should be circled.

Page 130

Graphic Organizer: Theme

Sample responses are provided.
1. The title points out the main conflict in the story: the bet between the banker and the lawyer.

2. The main character changes dramatically. The lawyer realizes that all his knowledge and wisdom gained from books is ultimately worthless since he will die one day anyway.
3. In the beginning of the story, the lawyer seems to believe that life has great value, but by the end he has decided that it does not have much value. Judging by the banker's actions, it seems that misplaced values often blind people.
4. A theme is not directly stated, but several themes are implied throughout the story.
5. Several possible themes are: Freedom does not ensure happiness; earthly rewards are of little worth; few people have true integrity. It does not seem like the writer is forcing us to accept a false view of life.

Page 131

Vocabulary Development: Column Match
1. b
2. e
3. a
4. Answer provided.
5. d

My Sentence

Accept any original sentence correctly using a vocabulary word.

The Modern World: 1900 to the Present Page 132

Page 132

Vocabulary

Underlined words should include "species that adapt to their environments survive, and those that do not die out."

Page 133

Vocabulary

Sample responses: Reasons include World War I, thousands dead in trenches, entire generation killed, war, weakened empire, and staggering loss of life.

Page 134

Vocabulary

Hammered means "worked hard" in this context. Reasons can include there is nothing being built here, three states worked hard to figure out how to have peace in Ireland.

Page 135

Vocabulary

Just means "fair" and the prefix *in-* often means "not." This must mean that *injustices* means "things that aren't fair."

Page 136

Vocabulary

Foreshadowed in this sentence means that Borges's work was at the forefront of a new literary style called magic realism.

In the Shadow of War Page 138

Page 141

Point of View
The woman is taking food to people who are hiding in the cave from the soldiers.

Point of View
Omovo sees that what he thought were the dead bodies of animals floating in the river are actually the dead bodies of men.

Page 142

Making Predictions
Since the soldiers were following Omovo right before he passed out, it seems as if they might capture him now.

Page 143

Graphic Organizer: Point of View
1. Omovo sees that the swollen dead animals are really the swollen bodies of dead men.
2. Answer provided.

Shakespeare's Sister Page 144

Page 146

Essay
Sample responses provided.
Reasons why it was impossible for any woman to have written Shakespeare's plays are that women did not get an education, did not go to school, did not learn grammar or logic, or read Latin poets. A woman in that time was not allowed to read but had to do household chores, such as mending stockings or stirring the stew.

Page 147

Identifying the Author's Beliefs
The reason the bishop was right was that women were uneducated servants all their lives. They had to keep working, and there was no time or energy left for writing, even if they had known how to.

Page 148

Vocabulary
Word to be circled is "pure."

Identifying the Author's Beliefs
Sample responses provided.
The special obstacles that women faced if they wanted to write were that no woman could have the privacy of a room of her own in which to work, she had no money of her own, she was not free to do any of the things that male writers could do, such as taking a walking tour or long journeys. Also, people thought that women writing was ridiculous.

Page 149

Graphic Organizer: Identifying the Author's Beliefs
1. Answer provided.
2. Women were married off at a young age.

3. Women were not sent to school, and they were even discouraged from learning.
4. Women were encouraged to focus on domestic duties, such as mending stockings and minding the stew.
5. A woman would not have been able to sign her work and bring it to public attention.

The Doll's House Page 150

Page 153

Symbol
Sample response: The circle of girls around Isabel symbolizes the unbridgeable gap between the classes. Just as a British commoner would not approach the queen of England, so the Kelveys dare come only within earshot of the upper-class Burnells. This is an example of the story's focus on social classes.

Making Inferences
Sample response: Kezia is not bound by the class rules as yet—she asks her mother if she can't invite the Kelveys "just once." Kezia's mother is completely bound by the class rules and does not even give a reason for refusing to let the Kelveys in.

Page 154

Symbol
For the upper-class girls, being a servant symbolizes something awful.

Page 155

Symbol
Sample response: The little lamp symbolizes the light of human kindness; it is a symbol of the life enjoyed by the upper classes.

Page 156

Graphic Organizer: Symbol
Sample responses provided.
1. Answer provided.
2. personal symbol; the most human and welcoming feature of the doll's house; also the light of human kindness.
3. the close upper-class society that the Kelveys can never enter.
4. something awful; a dreadful occupation.
5. hard, cruel words and actions.

Accept any answer that explains the symbolism of the place, thing, or event.

Page 157

Vocabulary Development
1. Answer provided.
2. It is a time to go outside and play—recess time.
   Explanation: The children go outside for playtime.

3. Else has a begging look.
Explanation: The second half of the sentence explains what she is begging for—she wants to see the house.

4. Aunt Beryl is calling out in an unfriendly voice.
Explanation: It says that Aunt Beryl shouted and stared as if she couldn't believe what she saw. This is unfriendly. Her words are unfriendly, and her voice is described as furious as well as cold. *Furious* means "very angry."